F*ck You Chaos

Declutter Your Home, Mind and
Finances to Discover More
Happiness, Calm, Purpose and
Abundance

Dominika Choroszko

978-1-7397562-0-8 (softcover)
978-1-7397562-1-5 (ebook)

Editor: Sandy Draper
Proof-reader: Polgarus Studio
Cover design: Danisha Asif
Interior layouts: Polgarus Studio

www.dominikachoroszko.com

DOWNLOAD YOUR FREE RESOURCES!

Thank you for buying my book. I'm giving away a bonus gift to supplement each part of the book to make decluttering and organising even easier.

Your free bonus gift comes with the following:

- Handy storage solutions
- Recommended mindset books and podcasts
- Easy to maintain budget template, so you don't have to build it from scratch
- My favourite workouts to keep your mind calm and body energised

And much more!

To download, go to:
www.dominikachoroszko.com/free

Follow me on social media!
www.instagram.com/theorganisedintrovert

For Bibi.

Contents

Introduction

Time to Make Life Happen for You, Not to You

Do you ever feel stressed, worried, or anxious, running around like a headless chicken, trying to make sense of circumstances that seemingly hold you hostage whilst simultaneously feeling like you're drowning? No matter how big or small, chances are you have complained about one or more of the following: *Where the hell does all my money go? Why haven't I got any energy? I need to get fit and eat better. Where the fuck are my keys? Man, this house is a mess. Why do some people seem to have it easy in life? This will never be me.*

What do all of these seemingly unrelated things have in common? We allow these thoughts to take over our lives. We talk about the mess, the keys, the money, how we feel, the food we eat and the exercise we do (or don't do) as though they're ganging up on us and enjoying making us miserable. It may surprise you, but here's the thing: it's all an illusion.

You may have tried to get on top of things before, only to slip back to old ways and feel even more frustrated. I'm here to tell you there are ways to make life happen for you rather than to you. Taking control and significantly reducing your stress and anxiety is not that complicated, and I'll show you exactly what to do to get (and stay!) on top of your shit. The answer to most of these problems is the one thing I do best – organising. I've been perfecting the strategies I'll be sharing in this book for the last couple of decades, and they will put you back in the driver's seat.

If you're wondering how being organised will help increase your self-esteem, reduce your worrying, or increase your income, I hear you. Being organised is often perceived as simply having a neatly written to-do list or a tidy house, but that's only a tiny part of it. Bringing order to chaos is a tool you can use to identify things in your life that aren't working and take action to get you where you want to be. So it's a lot more than a to-do list – it's a lifestyle. And what you'll learn in this book is a holistic approach that can be applied to pretty much anything to tame the chaos around you so you can focus your energy on creating a happier life filled with joy instead of stress.

Passion from Chaos

I became passionate about organising when I properly decluttered my room as a teenager. I say properly because that was the first time I poured my heart and soul into the process and did it thoroughly. I fell in love with how a bright, airy, tidy room made me feel. How I could always find what I was looking for and recite a complete list of my possessions. How energised, yet calm, I felt, knowing that everything around me was under control. There was a real correlation between the level of tidiness and my mood. Since then, I've lived by the following overarching golden principle:

Audit the present situation (identify clutter), clear what's not needed (purge) and create a structure for what you've kept (organise).

I've applied the above principle to every area of my life. Because when you *know* what's not working and become *aware* of what needs to be disposed of, you can do something about it, and as you start developing these new habits, you'll find everything in life suddenly becomes more manageable and less stressful.

For example, when I was a kid, I despised writing. I used to stare at a blank piece of paper, sometimes crying for hours because the clock was ticking, the deadline was fast approaching, and I just sat there completely overwhelmed, not knowing where to begin. With so many thoughts and possible things to write about, where on Earth was I meant to start? So I kept drowning in the chaos of my own thoughts until one day, I sat down and figured out an approach to tame the damn thing. First of all, I wrote down all the ideas that popped up in my head. Then, since there was a word limit, I prioritised the most important concepts and discarded the rest. Finally, I arranged my ideas logically to form a structure to guide me from the beginning till the end. The essay basically wrote itself! Approaching the problem in a structured, intentional way helped not only with that one essay but everything else I have written ever since. The proof is in the pudding: I've gone from being someone who cried at the thought of having to write an opening sentence to writing a book *and* loving the whole process!

And before you start worrying that this is about trying to control everything, there is a huge difference between being organised and being a control freak. The first one *frees* you, the second one *traps* you. This isn't about controlling the unknown and trying to predict every single outcome; that's simply not possible. Uncertainty is a part of life, and embracing it is crucial if you don't want to drive yourself nuts. What I want to share with you is how to eliminate *unnecessary* stress and shine a light on the parts of your life where you feel anxious or overwhelmed, even though you *don't have to be*. Those areas can easily be fixed with thoughtful consideration and a simple, intentional approach.

How to Use This Book

The book is divided into three parts covering physical space, mindset and finances:

Part I: Bring Calm and Order to Your Physical Space

Part II: Declutter Your Thoughts and Grow Your Mindset

Part III: Grow Your Personal Finances

This is because when you fix those things, you create more space in your life and unlock energy levels you didn't know you had – meaning you can focus on other things you may have neglected, like your fitness, diet, hobbies and even your purpose in life.

I recommend starting with your physical space before diving into deeper issues of mindset and financial health because that's what I've found works best. However, if you'd prefer to start with mindset or finances, that's good too. Whatever you decide, you might find it helpful to read to the end of the book before making a start and keeping a journal or notebook close by to note down ideas or thoughts you have as you read.

Organising these three key areas worked wonders for my happiness and overall wellbeing. After all, it's hard to be unhappy and stressed when you have a positive outlook on life, know how to save money each month *and* live in a home that quite literally caresses your soul! It's almost like magic. And if you're the type that tends to worry a lot, I hear you too. I'm a highly sensitive person (HSP), meaning my central nervous system is more sensitive to physical, emotional and social stimuli. As a result, I get overwhelmed quicker than most people.

On top of that (or perhaps as a result), I've suffered from anxiety since I was a small child, so it wasn't always an easy ride – particularly the mindset part. In my quest to stop my mind from self-sabotaging me, I worked hard to upgrade my thoughts and behaviours and achieved incredible things. I'll share the exact strategies I used in this book. Anxiety is all I ever knew, so I genuinely believe that if I could get my shit together and finally feel happy in my own skin, so can anyone else.

In working with others, I've found that sometimes it can feel hard to get excited about tidying up, doing mindset work, budgeting or refocusing our energy because they feel like chores, hard work or just some boring stuff you have to do. It's almost impossible to stick with something when you feel deflated just thinking about it. But the key to the success of my formula is that it is *sustainable* and *rewarding*! I spent years experimenting and perfecting staying organised, and now I want to share my strategies with you. I hope it changes your life the way it changed mine.

Part I

Bring Calm and Order to Your Physical Space

'You arrive at a village, and in this calm environment, one starts to hear echo.'

~Yannick Noah, French athlete

Chapter 1

The Easy Win

Why start by organising and clearing your home? Anyone can do it, and the results are almost instant. Once the clutter begins to disappear, you will feel more energised, pumped up and motivated to move on to your mind and finances, which we'll be talking about in the following sections. Once you feel the benefits, you'll never want to get back to living in chaos, and it makes it much easier to address deeper issues of mindset and sort out your finances.

You don't even need to be a tidy sort of person to achieve this. Was I always a neat and organised person? Hell no. I was a rebellious little shit, so when my parents told me to clean my room, I did the exact opposite. (I've never been good at being told what to do.) That is until I found an incentive for tidying up and discovered how much fun, joy and freedom it actually brought. So what happened? Well, I got dumped. You're probably wondering what that has to do with anything, so let me explain.

When I was a teenager, I had a mad crush on this boy at school. Man, that was infatuation central. And so it happened that he liked me too. We dated for a few months, and I was literally the happiest person on Earth. Overnight, his texts became drier and less frequent, and a week later, I got dumped via instant messenger. This experience brought an entirely new level of sadness that I had never known before, and I had no idea how to cope. I felt depressed, lost my appetite and a ton of weight, and could barely get out of bed. I didn't see the breakup coming, so I wasn't emotionally prepared to deal with it.

After a couple of months of total misery, I woke up one day and thought: *I don't want to feel this anymore. I'm so done with this shit. Okay, so what do I do?* But what could I do? I was just a teenager living with my parents, the internet wasn't really a thing, and I didn't want to talk to my friends about it because I didn't want their pity. I stood in the middle of my room, looked around and could feel myself getting pissed off. I needed to take my anger out on something and decided to take it out on . . . my belongings. I opened one of the drawers, and that's when I lost it. *A whole drawer of Legos? Really? When was the last fucking time I used it?! Oh, and that bucket of old dolls . . . really? And why the fuck do I still have that faded brown top?* (It used to be a child's T-shirt which now resembled a crop top on a teenager.) I felt actual *rage*. But for the first time in a long time, I also felt a flow of energy, and it felt good. I ran to the kitchen, grabbed a roll of bin bags and started filling them up with stuff I no longer needed or wanted. The more space I created, the more energised I felt.

A few hours later, my mum finally plucked up the courage to check up on me, and I still laugh when I remember the look on her face! When she saw twenty bin bags lined up in the corridor, she took a while to pick her jaw off the floor because tidying up was not something her daughter was known for - let alone on this scale!

Loads of that stuff went to charity, other stuff was old or broken and had to be binned, and all of it was hiding in my tiny room! Madness. No wonder I didn't enjoy tidying; with so much stuff everywhere, chaos would always creep back in a few days later, and I found the constant tidying laborious. When I was done, I remember sitting on the floor all dirty, stinky and tired, but lighter. Something had changed in me. I no longer felt deeply miserable, and all I could think was *Fuck! That was oddly therapeutic*. And I never looked back.

Today, I am grateful for the heartache from my teenage days because had that not happened, I wouldn't have found my unique 'superpower', as my friends call it, and my passion for organisation. This passion is literally oozing out of me, and that's why my aim is to help as many people as possible feel how I felt when I decluttered that room. Without exaggeration, it literally changed my life. Weirdly, having less stuff made me feel more abundant as well.

Think about it: you don't really walk into a fancy hotel room and think, *Wow, this place looks like a dumpster*. It's all very minimalistic and intentional. Everything has a purpose. Having experienced that feeling of abundance, I became very protective of my newly spacious room, which changed my outlook on buying stuff. Where I'd usually splash out on loads of new makeup or clothes I didn't need, I started to save my pocket money and decided that I'd much rather wait and buy myself something more expensive. I prioritised quality over quantity. This has stayed with me to this day, and every time I buy something, I ask myself whether I want it badly enough to introduce it into my home. It's almost like introducing a new boyfriend to your friends and family: you don't want just any old jackass to enter your inner circle!

Buckets of Benefits

If my argument for a tidy home still hasn't fully convinced you, there are plenty more reasons why you should get rid of clutter, so I'll keep going:

- Clutter bombards us with excessive stimuli which distract us from what we need to focus on, reduces productivity, makes it difficult to relax and can actually leave us feeling anxious, helpless and overwhelmed, according to psychologist Sherrie Bourg Carter.[1]

- Can you really be bothered to wipe all the items lying around? The more clutter you have, the more dust and allergens accumulate in your home.

- A clutter-free home means less cleaning. A Soap and Detergent Association study found that in the average home, getting rid of clutter would eliminate approximately 40 per cent of the housework – 40 per cent![2] That's mind-blowing. And in my own experience, having a clutter-free home means that I can wipe all surfaces (one bedroom, office room, kitchen, lounge and bathroom) in fifteen minutes. That's literally all it takes me.

- If you constantly feel like you can't find something literally there a minute ago, you're not alone. It is estimated that throughout our lifetime, we spend approximately 153 days looking for things we've misplaced![3] That's almost half a year. I can think of so many other things I'd rather be doing.

- Decluttering gives you an excellent opportunity to let go of your past. We often keep things that remind us of failed relationships or bring painful memories. It's time to move on.

- And finally, in a study by IKEA, 31 per cent of those surveyed reported more satisfaction from clearing out their closet than they did after sex.[4] (Okay, they might be exaggerating, but you get the gist: decluttering feels good!)

Your home should be your sanctuary – your sacred place where you can relax and unwind. And the best part is nothing stops you from having that premium hotel feeling all day, every day. We live in crazy times right now, and many more of us are working from home, so it has never been more important to live in a place that recharges your energy levels instead of draining them.

Chapter 2

Foundations of Tidy Spaces

You might think organising your space will be complicated, difficult, painful and require bullshit containers or putting stickers that say 'pasta' on glass jars (as if you can't see what's inside). In other words, faffy and expensive. I've seen so much rubbish (*ha!*) written about decluttering that anyone would think you need a PhD to crack the tidiness code. I'm here to tell you that it's simple, and if you follow the principles in this section, you'll be on your way to enjoying a clutter-free life, regardless of the size of your home.

Stuff-to-Storage Ratio

If you have too much stuff and not enough space to store it, no number of pretty storage boxes or containers will help you. You're just going to end up with organised clutter! What's more, it really doesn't matter whether you live in a mansion or a small room in shared accommodations; what matters is that your belongings are proportionate to the available space. Of course, as we get older, we tend to acquire bigger homes and more stuff. But just because we can doesn't mean we should. Whether it's overflowing cupboards and drawers or packed-out garages and attics, having too much stuff for the available space only leads to overwhelm. So whatever your situation right now, trust that you can find the sweet spot that works for you by following the key principle of organised living:

Have an adequate stuff-to-storage-space ratio.

So, yes, you need to organise what you want to keep, but that's the easy part. Before diving into the 'how' of decluttering, you might need to **identify** what's blocking you from parting with your belongings. Why do we cling to that holey sweater, that ugly ornament or a pile of old birthday cards?

Letting Go of Your Emotional Attachment to Stuff

We attach a full spectrum of emotions to objects. In my journey to live clutter-free, I've experienced all of them, so I know that getting to the core of *why* we hold onto things is tremendously helpful in deciding what to throw away and what to keep. Understanding your own deeply rooted struggles will help you more than a thousand checklists. Anyone can open a cupboard and identify items they don't use, but the reasons *why* you can't part with them are in your head – not in the closet. So let's dive into the key emotions that jerk our chains when trying to declutter.

You feel guilty

This is the big one. When throwing away gifts from people you love, you remember that your close friend or a family member spent time and money getting you something nice, hoping that you'd like it. So throwing it away feels like breaking their heart, stomping all over it and basically saying, 'I don't care about your gift'. In turn, this makes us feel ungrateful and guilty, so we suck it up and let these unwanted things take up precious space and collect dust. Of all the emotions, guilt is the most difficult one to work through for most people.

My loved ones know the one thing I adore more than anything is handbags. I've never cared for shoes or clothes, but handbags always light me up and bring a massive smile to my face. As a child, I had many bags, but as I've mentioned, I've learned to value quality over quantity. My taste has also evolved over time, and I have specific preferences, including brands, colours, materials, locations where they are made and even how they smell. So you can imagine that anyone attempting to buy me a handbag is pretty much doomed unless they know exactly which one I want. The irony is people buy me bags because they are thoughtful, and their intentions are nothing but loving.

I remember reluctantly deciding to sell one of my gift handbags on eBay. In my heart, I didn't like it and knew I'd never use it. My mind kept yelling, *Ungrateful bitch. Scumbag.* But I pushed through, ignored that voice and published the listing. Ten minutes later, I got a message from a woman asking me for the bag's dimensions and saying, 'Oh my god, I've been looking for a bag like this for

AGES! I love it!' As I was responding to her, another message came through from an equally excited woman. I was genuinely perplexed: *wtf*? In the end, one of the women snapped up the bag first, leaving the other one really upset. That made me realise something: because *we* don't love or need an item doesn't mean that nobody else will.

There is someone out there right now who literally wants the thing that you don't want. Someone who will pay for it, having looked at tens or even hundreds of other listings. Someone who will walk into a charity shop and – of all the available items – choose yours. So don't deny other people this feeling of happiness and excitement. Plus, don't forget that you're actually contributing to a good cause when you donate your items. So when guilt pops up, remember:

Giving away belongings you don't love or want will make someone else happy.

This works the other way round too.

A few years ago, I was looking for a new pair of jeans, one of my most dreaded purchases because *nothing ever fits me*. There are usually two outcomes: they fit my thighs but are way too big around my waist, or they fit fine around my waist . . . if I could pull them up any higher than just above my knees. I spent months looking for a pair that fit me (at this stage, I didn't even care about the colour). I dedicated a whole day to wandering down Oxford Street in London (introvert's hell) and was willing to spend a couple of hundred pounds. It was a fruitless trip, so I had no choice but to settle for my old jeans that were quite literally falling apart. Then, a couple of months later, I walked into a charity shop with no specific intention – just to rummage around – and found the most perfect pair of jeans. Brand-new, unworn Mango jeans. With tags. For the price of a cup of coffee. I couldn't contain my happiness! With a giant grin on my face, I walked into another charity shop and found *another* equally perfect pair of H&M jeans. Unused, with tags. Whoever donated them has no idea how happy they made me. They most likely hesitated before giving away brand-new clothes, but by doing so, they solved a major problem for me, and I am eternally grateful and still wear them.

Selling or giving away unwanted gifts has nothing to do with how much you love your friends and family. Their intention is what matters, and getting rid of a gift doesn't make you any less grateful for their gesture. Of course, you love and appreciate them for giving you something, so make sure they know it too. But at the end of the day, remember that **physical objects have nothing to do with feelings**. And if Aunty Margaret is trying to guilt-trip you for getting rid of that monstrosity of an ornament she gave you last Christmas, as harsh as it sounds, it's *her* problem to question and work through, not yours.

I think of unwanted physical possessions as a (metaphorical) punch in the face. If someone came up to you in Tesco, punched you in the face and got upset because you didn't like it, would you say to them, 'Oh, no, no, don't get upset, that was lovely'? Less drastically, you might prefer to think of unwanted clutter as a violation of your boundaries. It's your home and your vision. If clutter makes you anxious, overwhelmed or affects your mental wellbeing, you have the right to set boundaries, prioritise yourself and do what's right for *you*.

> *Nobody can tell you what you should or shouldn't keep in your home.*

Throwing stuff away is a waste of money

I hear this a lot. People struggle to part with their belongings because they believe throwing things away is a waste of money. If you fall into this category, let me ask you, have you ever been to a pub or a restaurant? I'll assume you have. Well, you could argue that you 'wasted' £30 on a meal that would have cost you £3 if you made it at home. I'm also guessing that you've been out for drinks before. You can quickly rack up a £100 bill drinking cocktails in a big city bar. Again, you drink at home and save a small fortune. Have you ever had your nails done in a salon? You could learn how to do it yourself, buy a kit and get twenty full manicures out of it instead of paying the same for one gel manicure in a salon.

I could give you endless examples, but the point is: you spent the extra money because it **felt good**. It felt good to be out having fun with your friends. Not having to cook and then clean up. To just chill and let someone else deal with your nails. To attend a fitness class with other people instead of doing it alone at home. Those things make us feel good and are great for our mental health. But so is decluttering your home – we discussed the benefits already. And you're telling me that you're not willing to throw away a moth-eaten T-shirt for the sake of your wellbeing? That holding on to the half-empty bottle of shampoo, which you're never going to use because it gave you an itchy scalp, will somehow save you money just because it's there in your drawer, pissing you off every time you look at it?

It doesn't matter if you're disposing of something new or an old item that you've had for ages. If you're not using it, there is a reason why and it's usually quite simple: you don't like it, it doesn't make you feel good, or it has served its purpose. So the idea that it's a waste of money to throw things away is flawed because it's not like you can magically turn today's clutter into its original cash value or get any benefit from using it. Therefore, you essentially end up with a dead weight in your drawers, which is worse because you're wasting your precious space.

Just to caveat, I'm not talking about seasonal items or suits or ball gowns which you obviously wouldn't wear to Tesco to buy your lunch (unless that's what floats your boat, of course). These are fine to keep unless you have many - in which case, the same rules apply. Do you like it or not? Does it make you feel good or not? If not, sell it or donate it.

It's also okay to make a purchase mistake. We won't always get it right, and fortunately, in most cases, you can return it to the shop. If too much time has passed, then you might just have to write it off. Shit happens. Let it be a lesson, learn from your mistakes to make better purchase decisions in future, throw away what you need to throw away and just move on. It's also okay for an item to have fulfilled its purpose. This could be old toys, clothes you used to love or old books and DVDs. These things have served you, and you're deeply grateful for them. They did what they needed to do, and now it's okay to let them go. Remember, if they are in a good enough condition to sell or donate, someone out there will be delighted to have it. If not, that's fine too - its purpose has been fulfilled.

I want you to consider one more thing on the topic of wasting money: the more clutter you have, the more likely you are to buy duplicates, simply because you can't find what you're looking for or you forgot you had it! So keeping clutter can actually cost you more money. And getting rid of clutter is an investment in your mental health and wellbeing.

Tip

Reframe the way you think about decluttering. Ask yourself: What do I value more? Keeping all this 'dead weight' and living in chaos or my wellbeing and living in a beautiful, peaceful home?

Sentimental items

When I was five years old, my mum took me grocery shopping at our local market. I always loved rummaging in the colourful stands full of fresh fruit and vegetables, clothes, shoes, toys, perfumes and all sorts of magical things. Everything was there - you name it. Just as we were about to go back home, I saw a toy stand. I looked up, and suddenly, everything around me stood still. My eyes were drawn to one specific soft toy: a yellow banana, half-peeled, with shiny black eyes and a big, cute nose. It was hanging by a gold string attached to its head. To this day, I don't really know what happened and why, but it was love at first sight. I simply couldn't imagine ever being separated from that toy. I asked my mum if she would buy it for me, but to my horror, she said she was a bit tight for money that month, and I had a lot of toys already.

At that moment, my heart literally shattered, and it felt like a part of me had died. I started sobbing uncontrollably and cried all the way back from the market, which was approximately a fifteen to twenty-minute walk. By the end of it, I started choking and couldn't catch a breath, but I kept crying. My mum was amazed because I never threw a hysterical fit. She always spoke to me like an adult (none of that goo-goo crap), and I was usually cool with the fact that there would be times when I didn't get what I wanted. But this was different, and she knew it, so we turned around, went back to the market, and she bought me that toy. Believe it or not, we've been inseparable ever since. My banana plushie has travelled the world with me, and thirty years later, I still smile every day when I look at it. I honestly don't know what happened that day, but the love I felt for that toy at that moment was real, and I just knew it would last forever.

Now, the reason I'm sharing this story is that I want you to know that it's okay to keep some sentimental items. *Some*. If you genuinely love something and still enjoy it now – keep it. But don't keep *everything*. I had loads of toys as a child, and I liked them all, but you can't keep stuff forever just because, at one point, it served you.

Most of the time, it's not about the object itself but what it represents. Often it's linked to fond memories of people, places or a specific time in our lives. I've also been guilty of keeping things that reminded me of great times. Can you believe that I kept a receipt for a can of raspberry Fanta from a Spanish supermarket for almost fifteen years? It was from my very first 'girls holiday'. I was sixteen, and my best friend and I took a bus (!) from Poland, where I grew up, to Spain. It was a gruelling journey, but we loved every minute of it. This was the first time we were 'unleashed' and had nobody telling us what to do, so of course, having smelled the freedom, we spent twelve out of the fourteen nights of the holiday in nightclubs, being an utter disgrace, drinking alcohol for breakfast and smoking cigarettes, even though neither of us was actually a smoker. We met some great people, saw unique places and had more fun than ever before.

So as you can imagine, every time I found that receipt buried in my wallet, I simply couldn't bring myself to throw it away. What I realised later on, though, was that these memories would be with me forever, and I wouldn't forget them just because I threw away an old, faded, stinky receipt. So I did. And guess what - that holiday didn't magically get wiped out from my memory. You get to keep your memories because they are in your heart, and you don't need clutter to remind you of them. I also found that in some cases, when it is tough to part with something, but I know it's the right thing to do, I simply take a picture of it but let the physical object go. A folder with pictures of sentimental items on your phone or laptop allows you to still look at them whenever you want, minus the clutter. It's a win-win!

Memories are in your head, not in a pile of physical items. Don't give them unnecessary power over you, and never hold on to anything you don't love or need.

To keep a box or a drawer dedicated to sentimental items is not a problem. It becomes a problem when you're determined to hold on to every single object that reminds you of something. Have you ever considered that by living in the past, you deprive yourself of the joys of the present moment? Once you create space, you'll be able to embrace the now, make new memories, and set yourself up for a happier future. Ruminating in itself is a type of mental clutter, which is something I'll talk more about in Part II, where you'll also find various strategies for 'mind tidying'.

You think you might need it later or regret throwing it away

Will you, though? How many times have you come across an item and thought, *Oh yeah! Forgot I had this! I'll definitely use it now!* Only to put it back where it was and have the exact same reaction a year or two later when you're decluttering again?

Ask yourself: Have I used this item in the last six months? A year? Three years? If not, then chances are you probably didn't even remember you had it and won't miss it when you throw it away. According to one LexisNexis study, it's estimated that we only actually use about 20 per cent of the things we own![5] There's usually a reason for that, so be honest with yourself. Is that skirt just a bit too big, those trousers a bit too tight or something just a bit off and you simply don't like it? Maybe you used to do something regularly or had a hobby you merely fell out of love with?

I used to keep an old food processor in my kitchen just because I went through a phase of making homemade almond butter. Five years had passed since I last made a jar, and yet, I kept thinking that I'd use it again. Eventually, I weighed up the odds, and the food processor ended up in the dump because, deep down, I knew I wasn't going to use it. And it was *so* much faff to clean!

One thing to add is that I have *never* regretted throwing anything away. After many years of ruthless decluttering, I only **once** looked for something I didn't remember getting rid of. I don't usually work out in shorts, but it was a scorching summer day, so I decided to dig them out. Having looked everywhere, I realised I must have thrown them away. However, I wasn't upset because they never really fit me well. I ordered a new pair which I loved and ended up wearing them a lot, unlike the old ones. So remember, in the vast majority of cases, you won't even remember the item you're contemplating right now. What we're doing here is creating your brand-new serene home and sanctuary where you love spending time. This is a lot more important than holding on to junk that you 'might use' (you won't). It's been clogging up your wardrobe/drawer/cupboard for way too long - it's time to let it go!

You might also be thinking that more stuff equals more abundance, but in fact, it's the complete opposite. Holding on to absolutely everything to the detriment of your mental health can indicate a scarcity mindset. This means that you'd rather overprepare than deal with a new situation as and when it arises because you worry that you won't have the resources necessary to cope with it. I'll cover mindset in more detail in Part II.

Trust your ability to cope with any situation when it arises instead of holding on to everything 'just in case'. There's a reason you forgot you had it.

You're overwhelmed by it all

It's incredibly common to feel paralysed by the magnitude of your decluttering project. In fact, this applies to every 'big scary project' in life, whether it's work-related, organising an exotic holiday, planning a wedding, writing a book, studying for an exam or anything else that requires time and effort. You look at where you are now, compare it to where you want to be and hello, procrastination! Simply saying to yourself *It's not that bad* won't cut the mustard because your brain immediately goes: *Erm, well, it is.* But what if you could just delay the worry and overwhelm?

My technique for when my brain starts flashing a long to-do list before my eyes is to think, *I'll worry about it when I get to it* and refocus on the *one* thing I need to do *next*. If your whole house is filled to the brim with clutter, you have children and a full-time job, and spare time is a luxury, you won't complete your project in one sitting. And that's fine – hardly anyone does! Whenever you find half an hour or even fifteen minutes, narrow your focus down to that one room you're working on right now. If that's still too overwhelming, focus on that drawer you're about to tackle. And if that is still too much, focus on that makeup bag inside the drawer. The point is to keep narrowing your focus until you hit that sweet spot where the feeling of overwhelm decreases enough for you to take action, which will be different for everyone.

Focus on the next step.
Only *the next step.*

If at any point you find yourself feeling overwhelmed again, immediately think of the *next* thing you need to do and force yourself to give it your undivided attention. In the beginning, it will feel a bit awkward and forceful, but the point is to push through that initial resistance and get you to start. Once you've started, most of the time, you'll find that it wasn't actually as bad as you initially thought. It's like getting your ass to the gym when you're really not feeling it and you'd rather stay all comfy at home. You focus on simply getting there. Then getting changed. Then your first ten jumping jacks. And before you know it, you've completed your workout, and you're feeling fantastic.

A few weeks ago, I was helping a friend declutter her spare room. She got overwhelmed a few times during the process, particularly when tackling sentimental items or finishing an area of the room, sparking 'Oh my god . . . there's still so much to do . . . WHAT NOW?!' Saying quietly to herself, 'One thing at a time. Just start on that next area and see where it takes you. Just sort through this one photo album' proved incredibly effective, and before she knew it, the whole room was done.

You want to fit into your favourite skinny jeans again

There is so much negative energy around this statement. If this is your primary motivation for wanting to keep something, you're living in the past, constantly reminding yourself that you no longer fit in your favourite skinny jeans or whatever that piece of clothing is for you. You end up feeling shit about yourself, and the last thing you need is sad, desperate vibes in your precious life. Plus, it's a superficial goal because self-love needs to come from the inside out, and we'll be looking at that in more depth in Part II. The whole point of decluttering is to feel light, energised, motivated and start fresh. Instead of getting hung up on an old pair of jeans, set yourself health goals without the unnecessary pressure. Prioritise developing a healthy *lifestyle* that's enjoyable and sustainable – something that will last forever and not just until you lose X amount of weight – and then reward yourself with a new pair of jeans. You never actually know where your new fitness journey might take you. When I got really into fitness and discovered weight training, I lost fat and became leaner but also ended up putting on eight kilograms of muscle! Even though I was in the best shape of my life, I couldn't fit in many of my old clothes. So don't let your old clothes limit you. Get fit and healthy, chuck out all the clothes that no longer fit you and reward yourself with new ones later.

To discover the new, you need to let go of the old. Let decluttering be the fresh start.

Chapter 3

Knowing Where to Start

There's a myth that you need to wait for motivation to magically appear to get started with something. In fact, it's actually the complete opposite: you start first, and the inspiration comes *after*. Have you ever gone to the gym not really feeling it, done a couple of exercises, got properly into it and ended up having a solid workout? Well, the good news is that's what happens most of the time, regardless of the activity. So, don't wait for motivation to get started with decluttering. Otherwise, you might be waiting a very long time!

Second, before you begin decluttering, it's essential to ask yourself: *How do I want to feel in my new home?* Like a badass independent bitch? Like you just walked into a fancy hotel room? Like you're in a trendy industrial city apartment? Do you want this place to be your cave where you recharge your batteries? Would you like it to be spacious and bright or perhaps dark and moody? Don't worry about what's possible or not - there's always something you can do, and we will cover the décor side of things in a later chapter. Think of your ideal scenario - nothing stands in your way. You can just snap your fingers and have whatever you want, so go nuts on your vision.

Close your eyes and imagine it. *Really* feel it. It's essential to have a dream that excites you and evokes positive emotions to guide you to make better decisions.

When I got my own place for the first time, I was probably the happiest woman on Earth because it meant so much to me - complete freedom; no more putting up with flatmates. I wanted to really celebrate it, so I spent a lot of time looking for décor inspiration, imagining my dream girl cave and feeling as if the whole apartment was basically hugging me, making me feel calm, relaxed and bursting with joy. When the time came to eventually pack up my stuff and move in, it was *so* much easier to get rid of things because that vision was so firmly imprinted in my mind that I couldn't just let some pile of crap ruin that for me by taking up precious space.

Lastly, you should aim to create enough space so that nothing needs to be lying around on the surfaces. For example, anything that doesn't need to be on the kitchen counter should go in the cupboards; your makeup and skincare products should also have a designated space in a drawer, etc. That doesn't mean that every time you open a cabinet, stuff falls on your head! Quite the opposite - everything should fit comfortably and be easily accessible so that you can effortlessly put it back where it was. If that's not the case and it takes effort to return items back to their designated storage areas, you'll end up with a messy home again very quickly. Hopefully, this gives you a clearer picture of how much stuff you should be aiming to purge. And don't worry about your home looking empty; you can decorate it later. For now, you're aiming for a 'blank canvas' to work with.

Tackling Decluttering Step-by-Step

There are two ways you can make a start: room by room (my preference) or by category. The reason I like the first method is that each room is almost like a self-contained project. You know you can complete it in a relatively short amount of time, and by the end of it, you'll have a wholly decluttered room, which will feel 'finished' and motivate you to carry on. I personally find it challenging to declutter by category (e.g., sorting out all clothes in one go, even when they are sprinkled around multiple rooms, before moving on to another category – say, makeup) because you end up turning your house upside down just to find bits from the same category and therefore temporarily create even more mess, which can be very overwhelming. Also, can you really remember where everything is?

If the idea of tackling the whole room feels too overwhelming and you find yourself paralysed by that dreaded anxious feeling in your chest, that's okay. Let's break it down even more. Decide which room you want to declutter first, get a piece of paper and write down *three* specific goals for that room. This could be:

1. Declutter the top drawer of my bedside table.
2. Go through my makeup bag and throw away anything that I don't use or that's broken/expired.
3. Tackle the left side of my wardrobe.

Now you have a very clear focus. This is your crème de la crème of goals. Forget everything else. Three goals might seem like nothing, but if you tick three things off your list every day, you'll be surprised how quickly your home will start to change. That's 1,095 tasks ticked off over the year! Hell, even if you tick off one or two – that's great too. By taking small steps every day, you train yourself to take action. When you do that for long enough, taking action becomes a habit! The more you do something, the more you normalise it, the less emotional you become when performing that task. And the good news is this applies to everything, not just tidying.

Break down decluttering into
smaller achievable steps.

Taking It Room by Room

There is no right or wrong in terms of where you should start. It's a personal preference. Ask yourself: *Which room do I really feel like decluttering? Which room am I drawn to?* Intuitively, you'll know where to go first. If you're struggling, here follows an outline of the order that has worked for me.

Bedroom

Since your aim is to create a 'serene sanctuary', it makes perfect sense to start with your bedroom, where you sleep, relax and recharge. Generally, it's easiest to tackle bigger items and ones that you're least emotionally attached to, for example, clothes and shoes. Starting with a drawer packed with small, fiddly items (say, jewellery) will make you feel like you put in a lot of effort. Still, the end result will be underwhelming compared to getting rid of clothes and immediately seeing a massive amount of new space. You need that 'WHOA!' reaction to help you create momentum.

Tip

There's usually a lot of clutter stealthily hiding in your underwear drawer. If you have twenty pairs of socks but only ever wear seven, you know what to do. Also, anything that looks old/faded/has holes/you didn't even remember you had it should be tossed. And you *really* don't need so many clothes hangers.

Bathroom

I think this is a good one to tackle next for several reasons. First, you probably won't find any sentimental items here, so decluttering your bathroom should be straightforward. Second, bathrooms tend to be smaller, which means you can sort it out relatively quickly and keep the momentum going, which in turn will help you see that you're making significant progress. Once you start seeing changes and how awesome it feels to have space and easily find anything you want, you'll want to carry on. Get rid of anything that's half empty and you haven't used in ages, anything that you don't like the smell of, anything that pisses you off. I once bought a shower gel that didn't foam. It was simply awful. I bitched and moaned about it after each shower instead of feeling relaxed, and I never actually felt clean. What I learned from it was that it's really not worth keeping things that drain your energy levels and negatively affect your mood. Life's too short. So watch out for all the little things that irritate you and if you find them? Bin.

Tip

Keep products that you regularly use on display, for example, on top of the sink or in a bathtub. However, you should only do that for things you use daily and limit it to one per category. For example, you don't need four shampoo bottles and five shower gels all at the same time, do you?

Kitchen

Kitchens are SO much fun to declutter! There are usually some serious gems hiding in all the dark corners of the cupboards and drawers. Kitchens typically take a bit longer to sort out, but you will be suitably rewarded at the end. Having loads of crap in your kitchen can actually make you reluctant to cook or bake. Back in my student days, when I lived in shared accommodation and my roommates rarely cleaned up after themselves, I often abandoned any thoughts of baking a lemon tart or a cheesecake. The idea of cooking amid other people's mess was enough to put me off. To be honest with you, it makes me tired just thinking about it now!

Tip

Aim for your kitchen cupboards to feel 'breezy'. Everything should be easily accessible. Think about it like this: the more effort it takes to retrieve something, the less likely you will use it.

Things to watch out for in the kitchen include food storage containers and mugs, as these seem to magically multiply over the years, and you most likely only need a fraction of what you have. You also don't need multiple pots and pans of the same size, twenty teaspoons or appliances that haven't been used for years and are now clogging the back of the cupboard.

Finally (a big one!), anything that's expired – and I mean absolutely *all of it* – needs to go. Think spices, canned food, rice, flour, pasta, medications, etc. I can hear you say, 'But spices don't actually expire!' Even if that were true, there is a reason these things are a few months or even years out of date; it's because you didn't use them! Do you really think that now that you found that jerk chicken mix which expired four years ago (and most likely has solidified), you're actually going to use it? You won't.

Finally, as you go through your kitchen cupboards, give them a wipe for that shiny and squeaky-clean finish to complete the transformation.

Office room

This could be a designated office room or any area you work in or have a desk. Clutter in this area is usually very distracting and overwhelming, which is the last thing you need when you're trying to inspire creativity or just concentrate. You want to be productive and laser-focused on your work, not distracted by stacks of paper, old receipts and all sorts of other crap. The only things you need on your desk are your laptop, a notebook and a pen. Put other items (i.e., stapler, sticky notes or books) in a holder or desk organiser, not just sprinkled around your workspace, collecting dust. I personally like to spray my desk with a pleasant-smelling surface cleaner and give it a good wipe before I start working. A fresh working area immediately makes me feel more energised and ready to start. And it's so quick and easy to do when you only have a couple of things on your desk!

The thing that people usually struggle with the most when decluttering their office spaces is documents– all of those old bank statements, utility bills, empty envelopes and who knows what else. The solution? Get yourself a shredder! Honestly, it was a life-changer for me when I went through my old documents after many years of just accumulating stuff plus a couple of boxes of old lecture notes and assignments. And here's the best bit: IT'S SO MUCH FUN!! I'm getting excited just writing it! You can get a good shredder relatively cheaply (make sure it's a crosscutting one so that your personal information is properly destroyed) and save yourself hours of manually tearing every piece of paper. And once you've done it properly, you never have to go through the whole giant stack ever again. Whenever a new letter arrives, and you don't need to keep it, your new best friend, Mr Shredder, is ready to help and provide some entertainment.

Tip

Instead of keeping a pile of things on your desk to remind you to deal with them, write everything down in your notebook in priority order or colour-code them with different highlighters. Now you won't forget about it, and the stuff won't need to be on display.

The last area to tackle

Whatever your chosen order is, my one piece of advice would be to leave the room or the specific area where you keep the most sentimental items till the very end. These are usually the most challenging items to part with, so starting with those won't create much momentum. What you want is to make significant progress, see the amazing transformation your home has just gone through and let that motivate you to keep going. By the time you get to the belongings you're most attached to – old ornaments or overflowing bookshelves perhaps in your living room – you will already be accustomed to throwing stuff away or taking it to charity shops.

Deciding What to Throw Away

If at any point you get stuck and are unsure what to do with a particular item, ponder on the below questions and statements to help you make a decision:

- How does this item make *me* feel? Not my family, partner or friends. Me. Does it make me happy? Or deep down, do I feel indifferent or negatively toward it? What's the underlying emotion that caused me to keep it for this long?

- Does it still serve me? Is it useful?

- Is this item worth sacrificing my home vision for?

- I'm doing this for my mental wellbeing – to feel less overwhelmed, stressed out and anxious. Is this item more important to me than my mental health? (You might be thinking, *Oh, but it's just one item!* Yes, but there will be another one after that and another one and another one and trust me, they add up quickly.)

- Have I used it in the last twelve months?

- What is more important to you: this particular item or the sense of wellbeing you'll get from living in a clutter-free home?

- Can this item make someone else happy?

Only keep belongings that evoke positive emotions – that make you feel happy, joyful, make you smile, or you enjoy wearing them. Or items that are a necessity and you use them regularly, for example, a frying pan, cutlery, a coffee mug, etc.

Even though the 'necessity' items are harder to get excited about, if you absolutely despise any of them, you should replace them. For example, if your frying pan is extra sticky and ruins your pancakes every time – replace it. If your coffee mug is too heavy and uncomfortable to grip – replace it. There is not a single item in my home that I don't like. I genuinely love my frying pans, my shower curtain and even my kitchen bin (more on that later). Replacing all of the utility items that annoyed me made a massive difference to my wellbeing.

How do you know that you've decluttered your home properly? If you've only tossed a few T-shirts and just mostly rearranged the stuff you had, it will get messy again very soon. However, if you've done it right, you'll feel such a difference and a flow of energy that you will *want* to keep it tidy. You'll think twice about buying new things and assess whether you *really* need it or not because your priority will now be your new living space and how amazing it makes you feel. You won't want to ruin that for the sake of some crap.

Worst-case scenario

When everything fails, and you're still struggling to part with belongings you don't need to keep, here's a technique originating from cognitive behavioural therapy (CBT), which I find very helpful.

As humans, we're not very good at coming up with best-case scenarios, but we've certainly mastered the art of catastrophising. Fortunately, many of those fears are entirely irrational, and we can see them for what they are when we take a closer look. Ask yourself these questions:

- Why are you struggling to throw away this particular item? Let's just say you found a top you haven't worn for a year, and you're now saying: 'But what if I need it later/regret throwing it away?'

- What is the absolute worst that could happen if you do throw it away? In this case, the worst outcome is that you miss that top and can't get it back.

- What is the likelihood of the worst-case scenario happening? Not very high. I'd say 3/10. At the end of the day, you haven't worn it in a year or so, and you're likely to forget about it the minute you put it back in your closet.

- If the worst-case scenario happened, would it really be that terrible? How would you cope with it if it happened? In the grand scheme of things, it's just a top. It's not a catastrophe. You could buy yourself a new, even better one.

- What is your main decluttering goal, and is it more or less important than the item in question? Let's assume that you want to declutter and organise your belongings because you have too much, and the amount of stuff you have makes you feel stressed, anxious, forgetful and uneasy in your own home. Your goal is to create a relaxing, calming and harmonious environment where you can relax and recharge your batteries. Therefore, what do you *value* more: the top or your mental wellbeing?

Let's quickly go through another example, step-by-step:

1. Reason for struggling: I feel guilty for wanting to throw away a gift from my mother-in-law, even though I don't really like it.

2. Worst-case scenario: She will find out and be upset about it.

3. The likelihood of this happening: She is pretty nosy, so maybe 6/10.

4. Would it really be that terrible? How could I deal with it? It wouldn't be terrible. It would just be uncomfortable. She might be a bit cold toward me for a week or so, but she'd get over it. I could, however, use this opportunity to establish boundaries and explain to her how badly clutter affects me and how much I need this to change. And if she can't understand my reasoning and takes it personally, there's not much I can do about it, so I might as well let it go.

5. My goal versus the item: My mental health is way more important than the unwanted gift.

The purpose of the above exercise is to realise that even the worst-case scenario isn't as bad as you think in most cases. It feels a lot worse in your head than it *actually* is.

Chapter 4

Organising Your New Clutter-free Home

Once you've decluttered your home and have all this amazing new space (isn't it just glorious?), it's time to organise your belongings in a way that actually serves you. An effective system should basically keep itself tidy with almost no effort.

Identifying the Clutter Culprits

Over the years, I have identified the key reason why chaos and mess tend to creep back into our lives, even after a solid decluttering session and how to fix it:

To maintain a tidy home forever, everything needs to have its designated place and be easily accessible.

It sounds obvious, but if you've decluttered ruthlessly and yet the mess comes back, this is the main reason why your efforts never last and you end up going back to your old ways. So let's look at some of the main clutter-causing culprits and how to banish them.

Optimal drawer storage

Clothes and underwear drawers are one of the biggest offenders. Remember the last time you did your laundry, folded all your clothes nicely, opened a drawer and stacked the clothes neatly on top of each other and a week later, it looked like something exploded in there? Two things happen when you stack things on top of each other.

1. You can only see the top layer. Since you can't find what you're looking for, you end up making a mess which you never tidy up because you have to do this every time you search for things, and that's a faff. You might do it a few times, but eventually, you get tired of constantly tidying and give up.

2. You forget you even had the clothes at the bottom. Have you ever packed up your clothes for a house move and found that long-lost top and said, 'Oh crap! Forgot I had it!'?

The trick is arranging your clothes, and everything else for that matter, in a way that you can see them. So if it's a cupboard, stack your clothes on top of each other. If it's a drawer, stack vertically in rows (a 'file' system). This way, you can see every single piece of clothing, and nothing ever goes missing. The beauty of this is that it doesn't take long to fold. You just fold it slightly differently depending on where the clothes will go. I do this for socks and underwear, which are best kept in fabric storage boxes because they're small and fiddly. This was honestly a life changer for me. It only needs to be done once after doing your laundry, and then every time you open your underwear drawer, you'll be able to see every single item, which makes life so much easier!

Tip

Keep shoes in hanging storage, either behind a door or inside the wardrobe. On top of saving space and providing much easier access, this also helps to protect your shoes from dirt.

Box up faffy items

Another thing to watch out for is all the tiny little faffy items, such as makeup, stationery, medication, bottle stoppers, seasoning mixes, sweets, skincare products . . . you get the gist. These things are usually best stored in containers, and my test for whether you should use one or not is: If you were to wipe the surface underneath, would it be relatively easy and quick? If your instant reaction is 'F*ck this shit', then the answer is yes, you need a container. Since I started using storage organisers for my skincare and haircare products, I'm able to wipe the inside of my drawers in literally five seconds (it's crazy how much dust actually gets inside!). I'd never do that if I had to take out a billion little things individually and then put them back in!

Think about access

Another key ingredient to maintaining a tidy and clutter-free home forever is:

Store the most frequently used items in the most easily accessible places.

Anything that is not needed regularly – whether it's utensils, cosmetics, shoes, documents or anything else – shouldn't be hogging the prime locations and instead be kept in less prominent places. For example, when it gets warm outside, move your summer clothes to the most accessible sections of your wardrobe, and when it gets cold, rotate it again so that your winter clothes are at the front.

My favourite way to store items I don't use often are built-in storage solutions. The smarter the space you can find, the better, and these days, you can find pretty much anything with built-in storage: coffee tables, footrests, sofas, desks, you name it! Also, consider utilising the space under the bed. There are plenty of choices out there, and you can either get a large plastic container with a lid or an actual proper drawer. IKEA has beautiful wooden under-bed drawers on wheels that come in various colours to match your bed frame. They are sturdy, look great and are affordable. If you're looking for a 'clever' sofa, I'm utterly obsessed with Nabru. You can fully customise your order and specify whether you want storage, a built-in sofa bed, type of fabric, armrest shape, provide the exact dimensions you want and more. On top of that, they actually look good and are very affordable.

Bring order to documents

One of the things many people struggle to maintain is keeping their documents tidy. However, it really doesn't have to be complicated. For the papers you use most often, such as those related to your home, car, money, doctor, etc., use a combination of expanding file folders and plastic popper wallets. The latter is great because you can punch holes in them and store them neatly in ring folders. Make sure you label them and keep them easily accessible, preferably in your office area. Documents that are rarely used, for example, old education-related records or warranties for various appliances, can be kept in box files and stored in less accessible places. My personal favourite for these is sofa storage.

Don't forget about digital files, as these can also get wild. Instead of having every file under the sun on your desktop, think of a few high-level folders that describe the main categories. This could be money, career, wellbeing, house, car, travel. Most things tend to fall under these categories. You can then create subfolders to help you find what you're looking for. So using the house as an example, you could make the following subfolders: mortgage/rent, utility bills, pets, photos of interiors. Think of a structure that's relevant to you. It should easily navigate you to the files you need instead of you having to guess or remember where everything is.

Tame cables

Finally, one of my absolute favourite finishing touches (which in my opinion makes all the difference) is to tidy up all the cables lying around on the floor. I never really thought much about cables (hardly the sexiest thing in the world) until I got my guinea pigs. Since they were going to be roaming around the house, I had to piggy-proof the whole place and hide everything they could potentially chew on - literally every solid object, with plastic in particular, which seems to be a delicacy. Once all cables were off the floor, I looked around in shock and went: 'Holy shit, my place is so much bigger!' Most large DIY stores have a whole cable management section where you can find things like cable-tidy units, decorative trunking, Velcro bands that can be cut to length and many more. If you don't mind drilling into your desk, you can also attach a cable tray underneath. You can find loads of different sizes and colours on Amazon, and they are perfect for all the monitor cables, laptop and phone chargers and any other cables that need taming under your desk.

Maintaining Your Newly Organised Home

Keeping your home tidy, providing that you've decluttered properly and got rid of the right amount of stuff, should be *easy*. The minimal amount of 'effort' required is to quite literally just clean up after yourself there and then; don't let things pile up because that's when they become chores! For example, make your bed right after you get up. Get into a habit of washing the dishes immediately after you've eaten. Fold your laundry when it's dry. When you take your clothes off, immediately decide whether they go back in the wardrobe (for example, jeans or jumpers – please don't recycle your knickers) or the laundry basket (that would be the perfect place for the knickers). News flash: clothes don't belong on the bed, sofa, floor, chair or kitchen table. When you receive new letters, process them straight away; put whatever you need to keep in your labelled folders and throw away everything else. Put your makeup back in its designated place once you're done with it. These 'tasks' take no time at all. When you complete them immediately, spread out throughout the day, instead of attempting to do everything all at once when it's messy and overwhelming, you won't actually ever feel like you're tidying. The only thing you'll ever need to do is clean the surfaces and vacuum the floors, which, without all the crap you finally tossed, will be a breeze.

Another thing to be mindful of to ensure that clutter doesn't creep back into your life is to stop flooding your beautifully tidy place with new stuff. You might think, 'Oh, I have all this new space now. I can buy more clothes!' But just because you can doesn't mean you should! If you need to buy something new, stick to the 'one in one out' rule. Every time you buy something, you get rid of something else. This principle is straightforward yet very effective. If you filter out what enters your home, you'll never have clutter again, and you'll never have to do a major spring clean ever again.

To summarise, here are the key points to remember:

- To maintain a tidy home forever, everything needs to be easily accessible.
- Use containers and storage boxes for small items that are easily misplaced.
- Store the most frequently used items in the most easily accessible places.
- Get into a habit of completing small tasks there and then; don't let them pile up.
- Adopt the 'one in, one out' rule.

There is really no need to make home organisation complicated. If you stick to the above rules, you'll notice a huge difference.

Chapter 5

You *Are* an Interior Designer (You Just Don't Know It Yet)

Remember when I asked you to think about how you wanted to feel in your home? Interiors can affect your energy in very different ways and transform the look and feel of the place. I don't know about you, but I personally wouldn't want to sit in an empty-looking home and stare at white walls! The good news is you can easily create at least a part of the look you like, and you don't need to be an interior designer to do that. Of all the things to do around the house, this is honestly my favourite part, and I'm *so* excited to share these tips with you.

Conjure Up the Image of Your Home

First of all, I want you to find an image of a room you like. Go ahead and Google it or find one on Pinterest. It could be a bedroom, a living room or something else; it doesn't really matter. When we look at images of interiors that resonate with us, we tend to appreciate the overall finished look but rarely understand what it is precisely that makes us go 'Wow!' The funny thing is, often when you take the room apart and look at individual pieces, you'll notice items that you may never have considered purchasing before. You might not even like many of them. But when you put them all together, somehow, they magically work and form a beautiful, aesthetically pleasing décor.

So next, let's go over the individual elements that make up the interiors so you can start analysing the images you like in more detail and really understand why you're drawn to particular interiors and not others. Once you've got this understanding, it will be easier to replicate the desired look in your home.

Think About Textures

This element is often neglected, but it is crucial to creating a balanced interior. Imagine a home that only has smooth and shiny surfaces: floor tiles, loads of marble, mirrors, glass tables, leather, metal ornaments, etc. This kind of interior would feel cold, uninviting and perhaps a bit like a hospital. On the other hand, imagine a room where most of the décor is composed of textiles and objects with a matte finish. Think carpets everywhere, fabric armchairs and sofas, stone, throws, fluffy cushions, etc. That's a very one-dimensional, flat look. Now, think of an interior that is primarily made of wood. I've seen a few of those, and they remind me of a stable!

The most beautiful, inviting, cosiest interiors combine different materials and finishes. We tend to admire these rooms without really knowing what makes them so unique. Take a few minutes to look at your chosen image and examine the interior with texture in mind. Notice the floor, furniture, decorative accessories, wall art, plants and their pots and any other items. I can guarantee that there will be a mixture of textures. Maybe a metal floor lamp next to an exposed brick wall, a smooth wooden floor with a fluffy rug, a fabric chair with metal legs or a glass side table next to a fabric sofa. Take a note of the combinations that you find appealing.

Choose a Colour Palette

Too much of something, even the good stuff, can throw your whole interior out of balance. Paint your walls dark and put in black furniture, and the place will feel depressing and heavy. On the other hand, purely light spaces will feel boring, monotonous and flat. The key to getting the colour element right is *contrast*. Even if you prefer lighter interiors, as I do, adding in a few tactical darker accents will really help you achieve a more dynamic and multidimensional result. Take a look at your chosen image and notice the different colours that have been used to create the interior.

Even if you have absolutely no idea which colours go well together, I'm going to share with you a technique that can help get your creative juices flowing.

1. Think of one colour that you'd really like in your room. Let's use teal for the sake of this example.

2. Go on Pinterest and search for 'teal interior colour palette'.

3. Scroll through the results and find images of different interiors (it doesn't matter which room) with colour strips of all the colours that have been used to create it. You should see a few different colour palettes, for example, combos that consist of different shades of teal and pink; teal, red wine and gold; teal and mustard, etc. This should give you an idea of all the different colours that go with teal and help you pick your favourite combination.

Now that you've chosen the colour combination that resonates with you, you can get more specific and search for ideas for the room you want to decorate. For example, you could type 'teal and mustard bedroom' and see what comes up. What I love about Pinterest is that once you've clicked on an image you like, it will show you related photos, which can often be a great source of inspiration and ideas.

I was recently helping someone transform her office room and used the above technique as a starting point. The room was small and served partly as a storage room for clutter and partly as an office room. Her vision was to transform it into her 'girly space', where she could work during the day and relax in the evening, read a book, have a glass of wine and just generally go there for quality 'me time' away from the family. The brief was more complicated because she wanted to keep a few particular pieces, so I knew I had to work around a grey-blue carpet (there was no budget to replace it) and a wooden desk with white elements. Another request was to create a poster gallery wall with images of fabulous travel destinations, inspirational quotes and things that would 'reset' her after a long day.

So as you can see, the starting point wasn't as

straightforward as having just one solid colour, but the technique I described still worked – it just took a bit longer. Initially, I did a few searches on a grey, wood, white combo and saved examples for her to review. She gravitated toward images with rooms that had a teal accent wall, which gave me more information for further searches. These led us to the final colour scheme: greyish-blue, grey, teal, wood, white, dusty pink and silver. We probably never would have thought of putting all of these colours together, which is why seeing actual examples really helped to bring it to life. It can be pretty surprising to see what works and what doesn't.

Once you've decided on your colour palette, it's time to find items in those colours to add to your room. Say you saw an image of a specific flowerpot that you liked. You can either simply search for it online by describing it as best as possible (example: 'white and black abstract face flowerpot') or screenshot the item, save it and perform a reverse image search on Google if you want to find the exact thing. The latter only works on a desktop, and you can find it by clicking 'Images' in the top right corner of the Google landing page. Now, this doesn't always work, but it's definitely worth a shot, and I have found quite a few specific items by using this method.

As you search, take screenshots of everything you're thinking of buying and dump it all in a spreadsheet to create a mock-up of your room. You really don't need any fancy software, and it doesn't have to be perfect. The point is to see all of the components, including any paint colours you may have chosen, next to each other to give you an idea of how the final result would look.

Tip

To get the right colour paint for your mock-up, I absolutely love a Chrome extension called ColorPick Eyedropper. It allows you to click on any image in your browser and tells you the exact hex colour code you can use in your spreadsheet for an accent wall mock-up. I like to fill half of the spreadsheet with that colour and place wall artworks on top to see what they'd look like in situ.

There is one other colour-related technique which I want to mention because it will help you keep things fresh and exciting. Let's carry on with the teal example and imagine that you chose to create an interior composed of white and different shades of teal. Multiple accent colours can go with it, and you decided to go for pink. However, after a few months, you get bored with pink and start wishing that you had gone for mustard instead. When planning my rooms, I like to pick three accent colour items that could easily be swapped later. For example, you could start with a throw, a flowerpot and a poster with pink elements and later down the line, update these three things to mustard. The great thing about this is that you can easily store these items, it can be done on a tight budget, and when you get bored with mustard, you can go back to pink!

You might think that your options are limited for painting and decorating if you live in rented accommodation. Well, they don't have to be. First of all, ask the landlord if they are willing to paint the walls before you move in. They will most likely only agree to white or a neutral shade – which is totally fine. A white wall is a great 'blank canvas'. There's a lot you can do with it, and at least the place will get a nice refresh. If, however, they say no, ask them if you could do it yourself, providing they refund you for the paint and anything else you'd need to buy. One of my landlords actually agreed to let me paint the whole place. Not only that, they knocked off a bit of my monthly rent for doing all the work myself! Not surprising, because it would have cost him a few thousand pounds to get the whole place professionally painted, whereas he only had to refund me £100 for the cost of materials. So it was a win-win for everyone!

Tip

You can add a lot of character to a room with a few framed posters to match your chosen colour scheme. For a more dramatic effect, you can even create a whole accent wall with just posters. Picture strips by 3M are a dream for this type of decorating because you don't need to drill the wall; they can hold heavy, large frames and come off easily when you need to remove them. They can also be easily cut to match thinner frames.

If you're renting a furnished place, you might have to get a bit more creative and find ways to include it in the design - just like in the office room example I discussed earlier. You might be able to upgrade a few smaller bits, for example, curtains, lampshades, shower curtains, etc. Many landlords won't mind, as long as you leave these things behind when you move out. Which, in my opinion, is totally worth it if, for the sake of a small investment, you get rid of a few monstrosities and create a space that you feel really good about.

Furniture and Physical Objects

Another critical element when deciding whether or not you like the interior is furniture and other physical objects, such as home décor accessories and plants. Go back to the image of the interior that you liked, and this time, pay attention to all the physical objects in the room. Spend some time on each piece of furniture, wall art, carpets, rugs, plants, chandeliers and other accessories. Try to imagine them in isolation and then look again at how they've been put together. You might notice that you love a navy-blue sofa and how it looks with all the black-and-white cushions next to a modern gold and glass side table. However, when you look at the sofa alone, without all the other elements, you might think, 'Meh. It's just a basic, semi-attractive sofa.' I mentioned earlier that this is often the case, so when replicating an interior, combine elements that work together rather than getting hung up on liking every single item individually. Because guess what – they will never be sitting there in isolation. They will always be in some sort of context, and you can recreate that context.

What else is your eye drawn to in your chosen image? Perhaps panelling on the walls? Are there any focal points or statement pieces, for example, a giant piece of art or maybe an antique coffee table in the middle of a modern living room? It's totally okay to mix different styles and have an eclectic room – that's what makes the interior appealing.

If you're planning to buy furniture, you really just need

to look at these individual pieces, find items that closely match the ones you saw and style them similarly. It's really that simple, and as long as you understand why you like something, you can do all of it yourself and don't need to be an interior designer to create your dream look.

Tip

If you can't or don't want to buy furniture at this point, there's still a lot you can do. Find images of rooms with furniture similar to yours and see how they've been styled. Then, replicate it in your room.

Layering

Layering is a simple yet effective technique that brings all of the other elements together. And guess what? It is precisely what it says on the tin: it's about building layers of textures, colours and shapes to create contrast, balance and depth.

One of my absolute favourite examples is a hotel bed in a really sumptuous five-star hotel. Why do people love hotel beds so much, and why are they so much more special than our beds at home? A hotel bed looks indulgent and premium precisely because of layering. Find a picture on Pinterest and take a look. You'll most likely see multiple pillows, some decorative cushions, a bed runner, and the pillowcases will often have a hemstitched edge for that extra 'oomph'. To finish it all off, these beds are always neatly tucked in and arranged very intentionally, rather than having all of the mentioned styling elements just dumped on top without a thought.

This is something that you can easily replicate in your bedroom. Even without going for the whole shebang, you can still achieve beautiful results. I have taken some of the elements of the hotel look to style my own bed:

- A white duvet cover with a dark grey cord around the edge and a stitched hem.

- Four pillows: two Oxfords that match the duvet cover and two with a grey and white floral pattern.

- One black decorative cushion with a white abstract pattern.

- A boho style throw in pale grey, beige and pink. The pink is part of the 'three-item' technique I talked about in the colour section, which I use to keep things fresh when I get bored with the current décor. My three elements that contain pale pink are wall art, a flowerpot and a throw. These can be very easily swapped out for pretty much any other colour as my bedroom is more or less monochrome.

To create a luxurious bed, simply mix different styles, textures, patterns and colours to achieve a more sophisticated, layered look. Elements easily layered include soft furnishings, wall coverings, home décor accessories and windows. Here are some ideas for you:

- Sofa(s) and/or armchairs layered with a few cushions and maybe a throw.

- A sculpture and a candle on a coffee table.

- A vanity tray with a few items you like looking at, such as perfume bottles, flowers and perhaps a candle.

- Adding curtains to your windows, wall art and rugs.

To bring it all together, look at a few of the images you liked and analyse them in the context of layering. Notice how the layered elements alter the room's mood. Imagine what the room would look like without it. There will be plenty of things you can replicate in your own place to make it feel more homely and cosy and create a space where you genuinely enjoy spending time.

Fixing Stuff and Feeling Good

We've explored decluttering, which is the absolute foundation in the process of creating a place you love (trying to decorate a messy home is like polishing a turd - why even bother!). We then covered the decorating part and things to look out for when creating a beautiful interior, so you're now well equipped to replicate your favourite style or at least parts of it. However, there is one other, slightly more functional factor that needs to be addressed because it will forever affect your mood: fixing shit around the house that annoys you. The little things that make you roll your eyes every time.

The whole point of using these principles is to make you

feel good, so your home can work *for* you rather than against you. It's great to have an opulent, layered sofa, but if you have a cracked toilet seat that pinches your butt cheeks every time you sit on it . . . that doesn't really feel right, does it?

When I moved into my current home, I had a clear vision and created an interior that I absolutely adore. But a few things were simply pissing me off and fixing them was the icing on the cake, which made ALL the difference. Here are some of the quick fixes you might need to do:

- Loose door handles: The last thing you want is for these to fall off, leaving you locked in a room. Check each one and tighten it.

- Flaky doors/woodwork: Nothing that a bit of sandpaper and a lick of paint can't fix.

- Toilet seats and bathroom fittings: If your loo roll holder keeps falling off the wall or your toilet seat keeps running away from you, it's time to upgrade it. I treated myself to a new soft-close toilet seat (hell yeah!), and now I actually smile every time I'm in the bathroom. Yes, that's right.

- Wonky shelving: Kitchen cupboards often lose the odd support stud that holds the shelf in place. These can easily be replaced with a wooden dowel, which can be bought very cheaply from a DIY store.

- My absolute favourite . . . the kitchen bin: It needs to be the right size, fit comfortably in the available space and be easily accessible. In my current home, the only place I could fit the bin in was behind the kitchen door. The problem was that there was no space for the recycling basket, and I had to keep it in a cabinet under the sink. That, in turn, was a nuisance because to fish out any cleaning products, I had to move the basket. Every. Single. Time. It used to annoy the hell out of me, so I finally decided to order a new one. I can't even tell you the joy and excitement I felt when it arrived! It's a beautiful, rectangular bin made with stainless steel and two compartments (no more recycling baskets under the sink!!!), and it has a soft close lid! And you know what? I fricking *love* my bin. It makes me smile, and it makes me happy.

I literally want you to feel the kind of joy I felt when I got my kitchen bin. There is something magical about having everything fully functional; it makes you feel really abundant. At the end of the day, can you imagine a billionaire's mansion with a wonky toilet seat? Nope. You might not be a billionaire, but you *can* have a home that feels premium. Look around your place and see if there is anything that you can quickly fix or improve. Think of anything that negatively affects your mood. You want to eliminate these things as much as possible.

Remember, you're creating your sacred place here. It doesn't matter whether you own your home or if you're renting; as long as you're planning to stay there for a while, you should be happy in your place and feel like you can relax. When the space around you gives you joy, it will be easier to organise other things in your life.

Part II

Declutter Your Thoughts and Grow Your Mindset

'A hallmark of a successful person is
that they persist in the face of
obstacles, and often, these obstacles
are blessings in disguise.'

~Carol S. Dweck

Chapter 6

Bringing Order to a Messy Mind

When you think of clutter, your mind probably isn't on the list of things to tidy up. It took me years before I realised that 'mental clutter' was a real thing and the degree to which my untamed, chaotic and negative thoughts ran my life, causing me unnecessary stress and anxiety. So I'd like to share my story to show you how it's possible to change your mindset and bring order to your mind - no matter how messy it might feel right now.

The Thoughts Come from Somewhere

Looking back, I have always been sensitive, and my earliest memory of anxiety goes back to when I was four and my mum took me to nursery school. When she told me that I had been enrolled, that weird tingly sensation immediately hit my stomach. In the weeks leading up to the big day, that feeling only intensified. Even though I trusted my parents, the feeling of the unknown terrified me, and from the moment I got dropped off at the nursery, I pretty much sobbed all day. The other kids seemed totally relaxed, whereas I kept pouring my eyes out for no apparent reason because nothing bad was actually happening! Little did I know that my anxiety, constant worrying and negative thoughts would get worse. Many experiences between nineteen and twenty-eight really affected my mindset, and I just let it happen because I didn't know any better.

It all started when I was eight and mum took me to a ballroom dance class. Weirdly, dancing came naturally to me, and even though I was prancing around in front of many people, it didn't make me anxious. Quite the opposite, actually - I loved expressing myself through movement. I fell in love with the sport, and over the years, my little hobby gradually became my passion which filled every spare moment. I'd be at school for eight hours a day and then train for a few hours in the evenings. Eventually, I started competing, which meant weekends were also dedicated to dancing. Homework was done at night or during lunch breaks at school because who has time for that. At that point, I had no idea that ballroom dancing would change the course of my entire life.

Every now and then, my dance club would invite famous guest teachers from overseas. I was particularly mesmerised by the teachers from England, the 'capital' of ballroom dance and dreamt of having unlimited private lessons with them. But the reality of growing up in Poland meant my parents couldn't afford more than one or two lessons at a time. I wasn't born into an affluent family, and paying international prices was a huge sacrifice for my parents, so I am eternally grateful to them for supporting my passion - even though at times it was incredibly hard for them. With the limited financial resources available and a lot of determination, my dance partner and I trained hard. We achieved something unbelievable: in 2004, we got to the semi-final of the Polish Championships and placed ninth in the whole country! For a dance couple that was pretty much unknown at the time, that was huge.

Why stop there? We decided to shoot for the stars and secure a place in the final (the top six couples in the country) the following year. So the whole of next year, we were on FIRE, trained extra hard and all we thought about was stepping on stage for that grand final performance. The big day finally came, and we were placed seventh - missing a spot in the final by ONE place. Not only that, we missed it by ONE mark from ONE judge. Words can't describe how devastated I felt. After so much effort and relentless training for twelve months, I felt like I wanted to give up.

A few months later, I was still feeling depressed. Then something unexpected happened. It was a summer evening in 2005. I was chilling at home and received a phone call from a dance teacher I'd briefly met a while back and had a couple of lessons with. He told me that there was a guy in England looking for a dance partner and that it would be a good opportunity for me to grow. Moving abroad is completely normal in this sport, especially if you get to a relatively high rank in your own country and basically 'run out' of suitable local people to dance with. The first step was to go to England and have a trial practice session with that guy. The trial was successful, and we formed an official dance partnership.

The deal was bittersweet: I would live with him and his parents, so I wouldn't have to worry about accommodations or food, and dance lessons would also be provided. On the other hand, I had to represent England, leave my family and friends, quit education (I'd just finished my first year at university) and move to another country alone at nineteen, with no guarantee that this arrangement would work out or earn me a living in the future. No safety net. Basically, I had to give up my whole life and bet it all on this, but all I'd ever wanted to do was dance, so, really, I'd already made up my mind. With no money for a plane ticket, I packed up a couple of suitcases, took a bus from Poland to England, and just like that – I moved.

The Breakdown Begins

Initially, it was great. Like I'd been cut out of reality and plonked in a dream. Lessons with famous teachers, international competitions, sponsorship from one of the biggest ballroom dance shoe producers and a dressmaker and invitations to perform shows in Japan, China, Hong Kong, Macau, Malaysia and Indonesia. I had grand plans and was bursting with excitement. I knew exactly what I wanted in our dance style, choreography and even dress designs (the devil is in the details; it's all about the whole package).

But the reality quickly kicked me in the ass, and I realised none of that was going to happen. I was an accessory in someone else's dream, which vastly differed from mine. It felt like I *should be* grateful for such a fantastic opportunity, and as such, I had little say in terms of teachers, the dancing style or even dress colours. I was even told *when* and *how* to clean my room, and as you probably know, being coerced to do something on someone else's terms and schedule all the time tends to have quite the opposite effect (and, of course, cause even more friction). I'm not saying I wasn't grateful; of course I was. I tried to comply as best as possible, but my vision was simply too different from theirs. Plus, I felt suffocated from constantly being with people who didn't understand me. This situation would have been perfect for someone, just not me. I am, however, grateful for the experience because even though I didn't know it at the time, it taught me two of my core values in life: freedom and independence.

To add to this, we lived in quite a secluded area, which meant that I didn't have any friends and nothing else to do other than train every day. I wasn't fulfilled, no matter how hard I tried to convince myself that I was. My mental health was taking a massive hit, but I don't think my dance partner and his parents ever understood why I was miserable. The reality was I was lonely, deflated, profoundly unfulfilled and depressed to the point that I almost completely lost my appetite and became detached from everything around me. My brain was foggy most of the time, and I didn't even realise I had lost ten kilograms until I bumped into an old friend at a dance competition. She asked if I was okay because my bones were sticking out. I should have known from the beginning that this was not for me, and deep down, I did, but instead of quitting, I sucked it up for another two and a half years. I was too stubborn and didn't want to be a quitter, so I pushed through the pain.

Sitting alone in my room, my thoughts became self-destructive. *You have no friends. Nobody likes you. You're never going to meet new people. Your life is meaningless, and you failed. You're so dumb if you think you'll ever achieve anything. There are many amazing dancers out there . . . What makes you think you can be better than them?*

I was on the verge of a mental breakdown and eventually told my dance partner that if this arrangement was to work, I needed space - or else I would go back to Poland. I needed to have some normality in my life. At least an opportunity to meet other people, be away from him and his parents and the constant nagging, and literally JUST HAVE MY OWN SPACE where I didn't feel suffocated and judged all the time. Much to his discontent, we moved out and rented rooms in two separate places. The move solved some problems but only masked the core issue: our dance partnership was not fulfilling. We were too different, and on a deep soul level, I knew we'd never make it.

Red lights were flashing, everything inside me was screaming that I should have left a long time ago, and the ultimate blow for me was that I started to hate dancing. The whole purpose of my life for fourteen long years was now the thing that I despised, and that realisation sent me even deeper into a downwards spiral. At that point, I literally had nothing else to give, and during one practice session in 2008, I blew up. I no longer had control over what was happening. My body and mind demanded a break and the words just came out of my mouth. I quit, just like that. I had found my passion - the thing people search for their whole lives - and in a split second, I had nothing.

The feelings that followed over the next few months were not something I had experienced before. It was as though someone had literally pulled the 'emotions plug' and switched off all my emotions; I was empty inside and just existing. Going back to Poland was not an option because most people never took my dancing seriously and didn't see it as a potential career. They'd always ask, 'When are you going to quit this hobby of yours and stop wasting money? There's no future in this. Get a normal job.' I knew my mental state was too fragile to handle 'I told you so.' So I stayed in the UK, but I had no resources left in my tank to figure out what to do next. At the end of the day, I had bet everything on the dance deal, had no education and absolutely no prospects for getting a decent job. What jobs were even out there anyway?? All I knew was dance . . .

Hard Times

What I didn't realise at the time was that this wasn't even the rock bottom - that was yet to come! With only £700 to my name when I quit dancing, there came a time when 'just existing' was a luxury I could no longer afford, and I had to go and actually find some money. Somewhere. Somehow. So I wrote a CV, which consisted of an impressive half a page (I made it to a page with a bigger font size and some 'generous' spacing), and started a tour around the local High Street, dropping off my CV in every retail store. Days and weeks went by, but nobody got back to me. At that point, I started to seriously worry about the prospects of becoming homeless. My room only cost me £200 a month because it was the tiniest thing ever (the sofa bed I slept on filled almost the entire room when unfolded), but what little money I had left wasn't enough to pay rent.

One day, I decided to treat myself to a coffee. (I know, you probably think that I shouldn't have spent money on an overpriced coffee, but at this point, I just needed to feel *something* pleasant, so it felt like a worthy investment.) Not wanting to go to any of the places where I'd left my CV, I walked into the one coffee shop I never bothered applying for. It was busy, loud, and I felt exhausted just waiting in the damn queue. I thought to myself, *Ugh . . . imagine working here . . . Fuck. This.* Eventually, I got to the till, placed my order and struck up a conversation with the barista. We spoke about some random stuff for a bit, and then she asked me what I was doing in England. I skipped the sob story and just said that I was currently unemployed and looking for a job. 'Oh, what sort of jobs are you looking for? Would you be interested in working in a coffee shop? You see, this is literally my last week here, and we're looking for my replacement. It's only a part-time contract, but there is an opportunity for this to turn full-time. The manager will be here soon if you want to wait a bit and maybe arrange an interview?'

Erm. Okay. Wow. I mean, what are the fucking chances? I was about to become homeless, so yes, I grabbed my coffee and patiently waited for the manager to come. I had my interview there and then, and somehow, got the job.

Working there was a shock to my system. Nobody cared that I used to be a British Ballroom Dance Championship finalist living a glamorous life (on paper at least) full of exotic travel. I was just a nobody who'd get into trouble if the toilets weren't cleaned properly. In my old life, I was respected, and now I didn't even have that. It's like someone took an eraser and just wiped out fourteen years of my life.

The other part of that reality was the sudden poverty I

found myself in. I earned between £400-£450 a month, depending on how many hours I managed to get. Having paid my £200 rent and other expenses, there really wasn't much to play with. I often walked thirty minutes to and from work to save the bus money. I also relied heavily on expired coffee shop food. Even though taking wastage was not allowed, it literally broke my heart seeing perfectly good food being chucked away every day whilst I was hungry! So as you can probably imagine, all of this was far from fun.

I would often just sit in the park on my own, staring into the void and light up a fag (even though I am a non-smoker), just to numb myself a bit. In the evenings, I'd sit in my room and drink wine. *A lot* of wine. My confidence was at an all-time low. I was completely defeated and started to feel that it would be better if I wasn't here. Yes . . . it got to that point. I felt like my life was meaningless and the thought of me not having been born felt quite soothing. *This* was my rock bottom.

Wanting to Feel Better

One day, I got so drunk that I fell asleep face flat on the floor in the hallway. I woke up with a dry mouth, feeling like crap and terribly nauseous. I went to the bathroom to wash my face, looked in the mirror and thought, *Jesus . . . you look like shit*. Suddenly, I got furious with my own shit. I was tired of how bad it felt inside my own head. For the first time in a long time, I actually *wanted* to feel better. So far, my life had been filled with negative thoughts, then a lot of misery and struggle would appear in my life, which in turn fuelled more negative thoughts, and somehow more negative events would always show up in my life. *Vicious. Fucking. Circle.*

I had no idea what I would do or how I would fix my shitty life, but I thought I'd just start with the thing I had control over – myself. I may not have complete control over the negative events, but I certainly could at least try to upgrade my thoughts. The thing about those thoughts was that they *weren't actually helping* with anything. I figured negative events plus negative thoughts equal misery. Therefore, negative events plus positive thoughts equal half the misery. I could choose to think, *I have no friends. Life sucks.* Or I could think, *I have no friends yet. But I like my own company, so tonight I'm going to stay in and read a good book.* I still had no friends, but seeing it from a different angle made a difference in how I felt.

I awkwardly started to force myself to stop the downward spiral of negative thoughts because feeding them was only pushing me deeper into self-pity. Some were easier to control than others, but enough was enough. Whenever a negative thought was persistent, I thought, *I don't like this. Get out of my head.'* or simply *Oh, just FUCK OFF.*

That was the first time I realised how flooded my mind was with clutter. The number of times I said *Oh, just FUCK OFF!* in my head every day . . . you wouldn't believe it! I had no idea whether this was going to change my life in any way. All I knew was that life simply could not be this miserable, and there *must be* something out there better than this. Fuelled by the slight improvement in my mood, I knew I needed to get off my drunk, depressed ass and do something. ANYTHING.

The first thing I did was tell people around me, 'I don't know what I want to do.' Literally, anyone around me who was remotely willing to listen, including the people I lived with, my colleagues in the coffee shop and even the customers, knew that Dominika didn't know what to do with her life.

Believe it or not, taking this seemingly unimportant step changed the course of my life in ways I couldn't have imagined back then. Things slowly started to change, eventually resulting in me picking myself up, obtaining a university degree, getting on a fantastic graduate scheme that kick-started my career, becoming fully independent financially and also attracting amazing and loving people into my life, which I'll share more about in a later chapter.

This was the humble beginning of my journey toward decluttering my mind and learning to take action. Even though I didn't know the tangible effect my mind had on my life, I felt I was on to something. It took me many years to realise that all the good things that happened in my life resulted from the thoughts I had about that thing. My golden rule then became:

Give your thoughts the attention they really deserve by developing daily routines to harness their true power.

Chapter 7

Becoming Aware of Mental Clutter

Most of us carry some sort of mental clutter. Some of it can be formed later in life due to specific unpleasant events, such as those I just described. On the other hand, many values and beliefs have simply been passed on to us by our parents or caregivers. As we absorb their words and observe their behaviours in the early years of our lives, our subconscious mind gets programmed to become the 'operating system' that will later guide our adult lives. That's when we learn what's 'normal' (according to the environment we're in) and develop 'setpoints' for different things, such as what we think our minimum and maximum income could ever be, whether we get married and have children, whether we go to university or drop out of school early, whether we go on holidays every year or never travel, etc. Unfortunately, many of these thoughts and beliefs limit us instead of helping, and often, we don't even know about it. We just take things at face value without questioning them.

Look at how many unhappy marriages are out there. So many people get married because they think they should but feel resistance toward it deep inside. They go ahead and do it anyway because that's just what happens. But why? I'm not saying that marriage is inherently bad. I'm saying that what makes one person happy can make another one miserable. And maybe it's time to get curious about anything deep down inside that doesn't feel right and question it. Ask yourself:

- Is this what *I* want?
- Am I being true to myself?
- Do I really need to do [*insert the thing*]?
- What value would it add to my life?
- What would happen if I did it differently?
- Would something bad happen, or would I be okay or maybe even better?

As children, we used to be very inquisitive and ask many questions that annoyed the hell out of everybody around. We were curious. So why not do the same later in life? Why don't we become curious about our thoughts and whether they're helpful or not? So decluttering your mind is exactly the same as decluttering a physical space:

Do an audit to identify what you don't need or want and get rid of it. Then create a structure or a routine that serves you instead of letting the untamed chaotic mess inside your head run your life.

Identifying Mental Clutter

The first step to making any changes is having *awareness*. You can't fix something if you don't know what's broken. It's like trying to perform a surgery without knowing which body part you're operating on! So the first thing you need to do is simply start *observing* your thoughts and how they make you *feel*. As you go about your day, notice the thoughts that cause that dreaded knot in your stomach. Thoughts that make you feel uneasy, anxious or negative in any way. To help you identify them, I'll go over some common types of mental clutter. As you read, just notice if any of it feels familiar and whether you recognise them in your thought patterns.

Tip

Don't forget to take notes. You might find it helpful to keep a journal or write down any observations you make about your own mental clutter.

Limiting beliefs

Limiting beliefs are synonymous with putting a ceiling on what you think you can do, what you're capable of achieving and who you are as a person. They are a funny thing because it's basically *us* putting labels on ourselves. It has nothing to do with the actual reality. Let me give you an example.

I used to label myself as 'unconfident', particularly at work, and find all sorts of 'evidence' to back it up. 'Oh, but

I can't really speak up because I don't know a lot about this subject. Other people know more than me. If I ask a question, it will sound stupid, and people will judge me.' That's the side of the story *I* was seeing.

And then an interesting thing happened. This woman at work whom I adored – I envied her confidence and literally wanted to *be* her, my absolute heroine – presented something blatantly wrong to the senior stakeholders. The data was completely wrong, and therefore the recommendations were incorrect too. When someone pointed it out, she just said, 'Oh yeah, I'll double-check that and review the recommendation. So, the next thing is . . .' The criticism was like water sliding off a duck. She carried on unaffected as if nothing had happened. After the meeting, she simply updated the information, put in (completely) new recommendations and sent it out to everyone. The vibe she was oozing was 'Meh. Not a big deal.'

Now, did this change my opinion of her? No. She was still an amazing person and still brilliant at her job. I still trusted her and valued her opinion. If anything, I respected her even more. I could relate to her more (we're both human?! Yay!), and it dawned on me that confidence is how *you* see yourself. Back then, if I'd presented something so wrong, I'd probably have burst into tears and had a borderline cardiac arrest. Then I'd sit at home, beat myself up and sob that I was terrible at my job. Whereas she remained confident, and *therefore*, people continued to see her as confident.

From that day, I started observing senior people at work whom I had put on a pedestal. I started to notice that, masked under all of that charisma and grand words, they were often chatting shit. Other times, they might talk for forty-five minutes without actually saying anything! For the first time, I could actually see that many of these senior people were making it up as they went along – they just had longer tenures under their belts. I absolutely love what Michelle Obama said when asked how she got over the feeling of being intimidated sitting at big tables filled with smart, powerful men: 'You realise pretty quickly that a lot of them aren't that smart.' So very true.

Limiting beliefs can be pretty sneaky and hide, so it helps to pay attention not just to your thoughts but also to how you talk about yourself. 'I got a new job! So happy! But clearly, they must have been desperate to give *me* the job, ha-ha.' You're seemingly making a joke, but the joke is loaded with an underlying lack of self-belief. You might even be saying it to someone to get some external validation, deep down waiting for them to say, 'Oh noooo, don't be silly, you're amazing!'

Many people also find it hard to accept compliments (I used to be one of them!). Say someone just told you they liked your handbag. Do you find yourself saying something like this: 'Oh, it's nothing . . . it was really cheap. I got it from a charity shop'?

Both examples could imply that deep down, you don't value yourself or think that you're good enough to get that job or buy yourself something nice, so pay attention to this kind of self-talk, as it needs to go! Similarly, like my colleague who made a mistake during her presentation and remained confident, what matters the most is how you see yourself. When you feel confident and deserving of the best that life has to offer, you will radiate that feeling, and that's how people will see you too. Just accept that you got the job. That's a fact; it actually happened. You were the best candidate, end of the story. Don't write your own scripts and assume what people thought because you will never know that. Also, just take the damn compliment. 'Thanks! I fell in love with this handbag the minute I saw it and just had to have it!' It doesn't matter if it was cheap or whether you paid a premium price. Neither is good or bad anyway; you spent money on something that brought you joy, and you don't need to explain yourself. You deserve good things in life just because.

Money simply represents exchange; it's neutral. It should flow freely and be both given and received. Spend the amount you feel comfortable with and doesn't feel wasteful, and don't explain yourself to anyone. And if you feel people judge you for your choices? Well, that's their problem. By judging you, they project their own insecurities and unfulfilled desires onto you. I'll talk more about preoccupying yourself with what other people think later.

Action

Take some time now to think about your limiting beliefs. Are there any areas in your life where you put a 'cap' on what you're capable of, what is 'appropriate' to do or who you are as a person? Do you feel like you *have to* behave a certain way? In your head, is there a limit, perhaps a specific number, to how much you think you're capable of earning? Do you put yourself down when you talk about yourself?

Ruminating

This mental clutter is a pesky little thing because it keeps you stuck in the past - something that doesn't even exist anymore! Whether it's something you 'missed out on' or something unpleasant that happened, you get hung up on the negative side of things instead of treating it as an experience from which you learned and became stronger.

I lived in some horrendous places during my coffee shop and university days. Images of horrible, filthy, overcrowded places filled with people I didn't trust had a tendency to pop inside my head just before falling asleep. My breathing would become shallower, I'd get a lump in my throat, and I could feel the fear as if it were happening all over again. But it wasn't! The mind is literally capable of producing these sensations just because we're thinking about something shitty.

These memories held me hostage and haunted me until I decided to take control. First, I decided to examine these experiences and see what I'd learned from them. And I learnt a lot. I became ruthless at negotiating my salary precisely because of where and how I used to live. Back then, I made a promise to myself that I'd never be scared in my own home again. That I'd never have to lock my bedroom door. That I'd always be able to buy the food I want. That I'd be financially independent and never have to rely on anyone else. And I kept these promises, so it was time to ditch these thoughts and start trusting myself and my coping abilities.

Second, I'd release these thoughts every time they decided to rear their ugly heads. I'd distract myself or simply choose to think of something different. I'd already worked through them, so there was absolutely no point coming back to it. It's done. The topic is closed. Next thought, please.

Another type of ruminating, which most of us are familiar with, is pondering what we 'missed out on'. A while ago, I applied for a job that sounded interesting and paid a really high salary - double what I was earning at the time. I didn't get the job, and I was pissed off, stewing in angry thoughts. What I didn't see then was that it was actually in my best interest *not* to get that job. It was far from where I lived, so the commute would have been a bitch. The team structure raised several red flags and seemed like a disorganised mess (and you know how I feel about that). The line manager didn't even turn up to my interview because he had to do something else 'last minute'. Some random woman called me instead and went straight into grilling me without even introducing herself. But why did it upset me so much? Because my ego was bruised. And for the sake of the bucket of money, I was willing to convince myself that it was a great job. Little did I know that eighteen months later, I'd have a new job that didn't raise any of these red flags and was much more suited for me.

Again, this type of ruminating is pointless because you don't *know* the reality behind that thing you missed out on. You have no way of knowing. Continuing with the job analogy, we are happy to imagine how amazing things could have been. Still, we have zero information about what goes on behind closed doors in that company. The people could be dicks, the projects could be boring, or the job itself could be lacking longevity and be axed shortly.

(The latter actually happened to me many years ago, and the person who ended up taking the job I applied for was made redundant six months later!) It may or may not be the case, but the point is: *we don't know.*

Regardless of the specific scenario, here is why ruminating is unproductive: that thing has already made you upset once. By continuously letting it replay in your head, you miss out on the beauty of the present moment. The past has nothing to do with your future either. It's done. It doesn't exist anymore. Let it go.

Finally, there's the 'positive ruminating' where you ponder the good things that happened. How is that a bad thing? It's not unless you're stuck in the past most of the time! If you constantly look at pictures of your younger self, dwelling on how slim you were or how good your skin used to be or surround yourself with a mountain of items that remind you of the time your kids were little, even though they've been fully independent adults for a while (be honest, are you still hoarding all the toys?), you might be stuck in the past instead of experiencing the joys of the present moment. This could be manifesting itself in physical clutter, which in turn could be causing more stress, anxiety, overwhelm and make you feel claustrophobic in your own home. The good memories are not going to vanish just because you get rid of stuff, and by letting it go, you open yourself up to new experiences, new memories, more joy and more conscious creation of the life you actually want.

Action

Can you think of any examples of when you ruminated over something? Are there any specific unpleasant events that keep coming back to you? Are you holding on to some memories perhaps a bit too much?

Self-loathing

It's okay to want to be a better person and work on yourself, but it's a very different story when you hate who you are or a part of yourself. I used to hate being an introvert, especially since joining the corporate world, because it meant hanging out with louder, more extroverted people who would make me feel like something was wrong with me. I'd frequently hear that I *need* to 'come out of my shell'. I'd get weird looks when I didn't want to socialise after a long day in the office and get pissed in a pub. And until very recently, I truly and deeply believed that I was the problem and everyone else was 'normal'.

I guess I never really had a chance to be in my ideal 'habitat' – a place in the wild where introverts roam around free and happy and do their introvert things. That, however, changed when the pandemic started in 2020, and everyone was asked to work from home. Most people despised the situation and wanted to go back to the way things used to be as quickly as possible. I, however, felt like a massive weight had been lifted off my shoulders. I felt at peace. I stopped getting pounding headaches from the never-ending distractions and office noise and became more productive. My work-life balance improved. My personal life started to flourish. I finally read all the books I never had time to read and became chattier and more cheerful. But most importantly, I started to love and appreciate myself and the introversion I used to hate so much. I started to see it as an asset that enabled me to go through a period of uncertainty and widespread fear with a smile on my face and feelings of joy and bliss.

Today, I am proud to be an introvert. I love having a handful of real friends, deep conversations, deep connections with people, a lot of alone time, and time for introspection, personal development and reading. I love sitting in my office room for hours and writing this book. This is who I am, and I wouldn't change a thing because there is nothing wrong with me. My 'shell' is fine exactly where it is, thank you.

I fully embraced that part of me. I'm a deep thinker and not much of a talker. Don't get me wrong, I love talking, and when I'm immersed in a mentally stimulating conversation, you'll beg me to shut up. At work, I talk when I have something valuable to say. I don't care about the ego and talking for the sake of talking or so that people know who I am.

We are all unique - thank fuck! You are special precisely because of your uniqueness. Can you imagine if we were all the same? Life would be boring as hell, to say the least. And I do believe that there is a happy place for everyone out there; you may or may not have found it yet, but it exists.

Action

It's totally okay to work on yourself and become a better person, but you should embrace who you are and work on the things you can do something about. Are you forgetful? Carry a notebook with you. Are you always late? Set the alarm thirty minutes earlier. But that's different from hating yourself or letting the judgement of others affect how you see yourself. Take some time to reflect on the relationship you have with yourself. Is there a part of you that you hate and need to make peace with?

Worrying and catastrophising

This one is equally as bad as rumination in that you're worrying about something that doesn't exist, but this time it's set in the future.

As someone anxious since childhood, I used to worry ALL THE TIME. Even when things were going well and there was nothing to worry about! There was a time when everything in my life aligned for me: I had just been accepted on an amazing graduate scheme; found new accommodations that I really liked; found out that I had some shares in the coffee shop I worked for, which I didn't know about, so I cashed it in and took two months off between jobs to rest and get my driving license; and for the first time in my life, I was in a functional relationship with a normal guy. So what does my brain do? *It's too good to be true. Something bad will surely happen. You'll get cancer. They will change their mind and call off your graduate scheme. You'll be homeless. You'll crash your car during driving lessons.* And many other things I'm now embarrassed to even mention.

For many of us, worrying is just a part of our daily lives. We worry about our future, retirement, health, people we love, safety, work, money, job security, relationships and all sorts of other things. Even after I got serious about personal development and cleared out all the mess that went on inside my head, I found it very difficult to just stop worrying. *I mean . . . HOW?* For a long time, it was simply beyond me how someone could just *decide* that they'd stop worrying. Unconvinced, I'd mock these people and think to myself: *Oh, you've decided, and now you're fixed, just like that. Cool story, bro.*

One day, I read Bob Proctor's book, *12 Power Principles for Success,* and something he said really resonated with me: 'There is no situation that isn't made worse by worry. Worry never solves anything. Worry never prevents anything. Worry never heals anything. Worry serves only one purpose: it makes matters worse.'[6] I mean, we all kind of know that. This isn't rocket science. No crazy new information. Yet, reading these words was quite powerful because suddenly, it became jarring just how ridiculous the concept of worrying really is.

Think about it: if you're currently finding yourself in an undesirable situation, worrying is not actually going to *get you out of it.* If things are already shitty on the outside, it will just make it shitty on the inside as well! To actually solve a problem, you need to approach it calmly with a clear mind. How many times did you have a genius idea whilst running around like a headless chicken, hyperventilating and on the verge of a panic attack? Probably not many. Also, how often did you say to yourself: *Man, I'm so glad I worried senseless. I wish I'd worried more!*

Convinced that there was something to it, I started examining my worries as and when they arose, asked myself: *Is there any evidence that the thing I'm worried about is definitely going to happen? No. Is it 100 per cent confirmed and set in stone? Also no.* I might argue with myself, *'Well, but even if there is a 0.001 per cent chance, that's still a chance that it could happen.' Yes, but so could many other things. Are you going to sit there and worry about each one of them? You'd probably never leave the house. Also, if you're considering such small probabilities, why don't you look at the other end of the spectrum and 'worry' about winning a lottery or meeting your dream partner next time you do your grocery shopping? As harsh as it sounds, you're choosing to catastrophise, but somehow you selectively ignore the possible positive outcomes. How convenient.*

Since that realisation dawned on me, I've noticed my worries as they appear and significantly reduced the number of things I worry about. It didn't happen overnight, but the more I practised, the better it got. I promise you can do it too. You won't notice a drastic change because it takes time to develop new healthy habits. It will be gradual, but one day you'll realise, *Shit, when was the last time I really worried?* I'll talk more about addressing and replacing negative thoughts and worries in the next chapter.

Action

Keep your journal or notepad nearby and take note of any worries. Ask yourself whether they are logical or not. Start seeing fears logically and rationally for what they actually are: a waste of time.

Self-pity and overindulgence in pain

There were a few occasions in my life where I allowed self-pity to consume me. When I got dumped, when my job applications were rejected or when I hit rock bottom, working at the coffee shop, drowning my sorrow in wine and listening to sad songs about broken hearts. I was self-absorbed, bitter and feeding on my own misery.

The fucked-up thing was that as much as I hated being miserable, a tiny (TINY) part of me actually enjoyed it. Because by overindulging in my misery, I gave myself permission to do fuck all about my situation. Telling myself, *Things are bad. I am lonely. Nobody loves me. I hate my job. I have no money. It's not my fault. Can't do anything about it. Wah!* In a way, it's easier to just sit there and feel sorry for yourself instead of focusing on taking control of your life, which might actually require some work.

Now, it's okay to feel sadness, anger or disappointment, and it's healthy to feel these emotions instead of repressing them. But it matters what you do next. Are you willing to accept that the current situation is not ideal, reflect on it, admit to yourself if you made a mistake and look for ways to move forward or are you going to sit in your bed all day with greasy hair and cry into a tub of ice cream whilst going through the list of your misfortunes over and over again? The first one is self-compassion, and it's *productive*. The latter is self-pity, and it's not productive at all. It's demoralising and doesn't promote growth.

Let's say you didn't get your dream job. Consider the below scenarios.

Scenario 1: *That's it, I won't get another opportunity like this. I knew this was going to happen. Why bother applying. They probably decided way before who was going to get this job anyway. It was perhaps an internal candidate, and they just needed to tick a box to show they interviewed more people. That's just the way things work these days. I won't bother again. Fucking joke.*

Scenario 2: *It sucks I didn't get this job. It sounded terrific, so I'm disappointed. But in hindsight, there were a few questions that I could have answered better. I don't know whether it would have made any difference to the outcome or not, but I will go over my answers again so, if the same questions come up in other interviews, I'll be much better prepared. I'll take some time to relax and recharge my batteries today and will resume my job search tomorrow. Surely there must be better opportunities out there. This one just wasn't meant for me.*

In the first scenario, it's all doom and gloom, and there's nothing vaguely motivating about this way of thinking. Feeling sorry for yourself for a prolonged period and stewing in your misery won't change that you didn't get the job. The second way, however, is self-reflective, action-oriented, and keeps you focused on possibilities rather than the shit that already happened. I get it. You will come across situations in your life that simply suck and are not your fault. But you can always choose to focus on the things you *can* control and how you can move forward.

Preoccupying yourself with what other people think

I used to worry a lot about what people thought of me, bend over backwards for people who didn't value my friendship as much as I valued theirs and force myself to do things I didn't want to do just to please others. If someone hurt my feelings, I'd brush it off and say to myself that I was being overly sensitive. When a colleague or acquaintance whom I wasn't great friends with invited me on a night out, I'd spend money I didn't want to spend to go to a party I didn't want to go to or have the energy to go to and spend hours waiting for the ordeal to be over, just to be exhausted the whole of next day. When an alcoholic boyfriend embarrassed me yet again, drunkenly fell on the floor in a pub at eleven a.m. or picked a fight with a kebab shop owner, I'd keep forgiving him for two years, even though his promises meant nothing. He was never going to get help and change. When a manager asked me to pick up another project, even though I was already tired and overworked, I'd say yes and work even longer hours. But then, I started questioning things. Something just didn't feel right.

- Why do we give others *so much* power over us?
- Why *should* we do certain things?
- Why is it that we prioritise someone else's feelings over ours?
- Why are *their* wishes more important?

Well, guess what - they aren't. We are all human, we are all equal, and you deserve to be happy just because. And anytime you say I *should* be doing something, the underlying message is *I don't actually want to do it*. This will sound really harsh, but one day we're all going to die. Not just that – at some point, the Earth will cease to exist. There will be no legacy. There will be nobody to remember us. Some might say, well, so what's the fucking point? But I'm choosing to use this as fuel to fill my time with as much joy and fun as I possibly can. Whenever I'm doing things I don't want to do, I'm wasting precious time. I don't know about you, but I don't want to use the little time I have being someone's pushover.

Bear in mind that there are people who don't and won't ever like you despite your efforts. Sometimes even *because* of your efforts which, if too intense, can make you come across as needy and desperate. There are also people out there who can smell your weakness and will use it to their advantage without giving anything back. Now, you don't need *everyone* to like you; that's also an unrealistic expectation. Think about it ... Do *you* like absolutely everyone around you? No. Should they be locking themselves in their bedroom and sobbing all day? You only need quality people in your life, and those people tend to be drawn to others who have self-respect and healthy boundaries. How can others respect you if you don't respect yourself?

I now acknowledge that I won't please everybody, but that's totally fine. In fact, I am fully aware that I have what my friends call 'a resting bitch face' and that I repel many people. Awesome! The people I love the most in my life saw past it and were drawn to me anyway. The vibe I'm oozing these days is don't waste my time and don't fuck with me. I'm only open to quality relationships in my life, even if it's just with a handful of people, and I'm unavailable for bullshit. It took some time and practice and was uncomfortable initially, but I no longer accept things in life that don't meet my standards, I am not afraid to drop 'friends' from my life if they hurt or betray me, and I say no at work.

Recognise that to be truly happy, you can't be emotionally dependent on other people and addicted to what they think of you.

Because that's essentially what it is - it's an emotional addiction that needs to be challenged. As long as you're emotionally dependent on others, you won't be truly happy. What really matters is what *you* think of yourself.

Action

Whenever you're faced with a dilemma, where you have to choose between doing what you want and what someone else wants you to do, it helps to get some perspective. Imagine that one of your best friends is in your situation. You obviously love your friend, so what would you tell them to do? We tend to give our best advice to others whilst being ridiculously harsh on ourselves. At the end of the day, you *are* your friend, so start loving yourself more and taking your own advice.

Now, I'm not saying you should never compromise. There's indeed a happy place between being a doormat and being a dick. You just need to establish your 'negotiables' (things that are perhaps temporarily inconvenient but overall not a big deal) and 'non-negotiables' (things which, if compromised, will make you unhappy and reduce the overall satisfaction you're getting out of life). To illustrate this point, there is a big difference between taking on a one-off extra task to help out a colleague who is currently drowning at work and allowing your boyfriend to emotionally manipulate you.

It's not selfish to prioritise yourself. You have finite energy levels (for my fellow introverts, these are even lower), so you need to think carefully about what you want to spend it on and prioritise ruthlessly. Think of your energy levels as a pie chart: you only have a limited amount during the day, so you need to allocate it to things that matter to you. Plus, if you spend all your energy on things that drain you, you're not really in a position to be of service to the people you love. You can't give your best if you're not at your best.

If in doubt, always turn inwards. Deep down, you always know what the right thing to do is. You just choose to ignore it because the truth is often inconvenient. The vast majority of personal development is indeed about acknowledging your heart's desires and tuning to your intuition - being in true alignment with who you are at your core.

Finally, there's a facet of preoccupying yourself with what others think of you, which sneakily manifests in seeking approval. Many of us look for external validation or confirmation that we're on the right path. For your mum to tell you that you should apply for this job. For your friend to tell you, 'You're awesome, you can do this.' Why?

Because deep down, we don't believe in ourselves and need someone else to validate us. So if this applies to you, spend some time reflecting on this, digging deeper and asking yourself some uncomfortable questions because you're about to discover some juicy mental clutter!

Comparing yourself to others

This one is really a subcategory of limiting beliefs, but I want to bring it to your attention because it tends to be well-camouflaged. We often compare ourselves to others, both at work and in our personal lives. We look at another person and think, *She's so much smarter/prettier/funnier than me. She presents so much better than me, and she's just so confident. I wish I was like that. Her relationship is just perfect, whereas I'm single. Of course, she just bought another house, whereas I'm still renting this tiny little shithole.* You get the gist.

It's not just about directly comparing yourself to others, but also the subtle feelings of envy and jealousy. That feeling when your friend is telling you how ecstatic they are because X happened, and you try to be happy for them because you love them to bits, but deep down, you have that weird feeling in your stomach.

These thoughts and feelings are linked to limiting beliefs because if you truly believed you could have all those things, you wouldn't feel bad looking at someone who already has them. I remember years ago when I was single and *desperate* (ew!) to be in a relationship, every time one of my friends mentioned her boyfriend, it would hit a nerve for me, and I'd feel the lack in my life. This is why it really helps to fish out all of these thoughts and situations linked to the feelings of envy because they tell us *a lot* about limiting beliefs we may not even know we have.

I see things differently now. I don't have everything I want in my life, but that's okay – life would be boring if we didn't have goals and dreams. I find it exciting to watch how the more I work on my mindset, the more I achieve. Think to yourself: *Hmm, how far can I push it?* Simply have fun with it. I now see the future and uncertainty as exciting – almost like being a kid and waiting for Santa to bring me something cool (*what is it going to be this time?*) – and I love watching how the unknown unfolds.

Action

Of course, shitty thoughts will still come up sometimes – nobody is 100 per cent immune to it. But anytime you catch yourself feeling jealous or comparing yourself to others, refocus on *yourself*. They have their own timeline, circumstances, skills and resources, and you have yours. We are all very different, so comparing apples with oranges is simply a waste of time!

Mental Audit

Now that you've got a better idea of the main types of mental clutter that could be messing with you, it's time to do an audit. Go over each category and write down all the thoughts, beliefs and behaviours that are not working in your best interests. Identify the unproductive, useless ones that simply make you feel bad. Sit down and think of as many as you can and write them down in your journal or notepad.

More importantly, from now on, practise noticing these thoughts throughout the day, every day, and if anything new comes up, add it to your list. This will eventually become a habit, and you will automatically notice intrusive thoughts as and when they appear. In the beginning, however, you might want to put a few reminders around the house. Write 'Observe your thoughts' on a few sticky notes and leave one in every room. It really makes a difference because, in the beginning, you might still be prone to be getting carried away with negative thoughts without even realising! Seeing a reminder to check what's on your mind will often cause you to realise, *Damn, I was literally ruminating just now!*

The key to change is awareness, so one of the principles of cleaning mental clutter is:

The more self-aware you become, the better.

In the next chapter, we'll talk about ways to sort through all this mental clutter and choose the ones that resonate with you the most.

Chapter 8

The Powerful Mind

When I started my mindset improvement journey years ago, back in my coffee shop days, I didn't have a structured approach and didn't really know what I was doing. I just figured that the mind was the only thing I could at least try to influence when everything around me was a mess I couldn't control. Remember:

Negative events + positive thoughts = half the misery

And even though, after all these years, I already knew how powerful the mind could be, 2020 really solidified it for me.

Three or four weeks into the pandemic, I had my first ever panic attack. I don't know exactly what triggered it, but if I was to give it a wild guess, things had been piling up. I was worried about my loved ones who had underlying health problems. Other people's fear and worry were quite palpable, and it started to get to me too. One of my close relatives said, 'If I get Covid, I know I'll die,' which was ridiculous and not based on any science whatsoever but added to my own stress. Not knowing what the travel situation would be and whether I could fly to Poland for my nan's ninetieth birthday. Not being able to buy fucking toilet roll. Colleagues panicking and speculating about job losses. The underlying feeling I'd had for a long time was that there must be more to life and that I wasn't living my true purpose. Feeling like I was wasting time but not knowing what to do about it. The news on TV being all doom and gloom. Someone's 'amazing' idea to start showing *Contagion* on TV (*really?*).

Eventually, my 'bucket' got full. I suffer from anxiety-related breathing difficulties, but usually, I manage it pretty well. This time, however, the tightness in my chest just wouldn't go away, and after a couple of days of struggling to breathe, I was exhausted. It was the weekend, and my partner and I had loads of fun together, which distracted me for a bit, but when we went to bed, I kept tossing and turning because the 'belt' around my chest was slowly becoming unbearable. Around three a.m., I got up and started walking up and down the hallway and then went back to bed, hoping that I'd eventually fall asleep. My partner heard me wiggling around and woke up; he knew something was wrong and asked if I was okay. And then all hell broke loose. The new, unfamiliar feeling scared the shit out of me, and that, combined with exhaustion and complete lack of control over what was happening to my body, was the final straw. I burst into tears and, desperately gasping for air, told him that I couldn't breathe. The more I fought it, the more I struggled to breathe. We got up and went to the kitchen, where he tried to calm me down, but nothing worked.

I genuinely thought that was it – I thought that was the day I was going to die. So what do you do when you think you're dying? You Google it. I started reading the first article on shortness of breath and panic attacks. (All that with tears and snot running down my face and seemingly no oxygen in my lungs.) And the explanation for what apparently was happening in my body piqued my curiosity.

First of all, the article reassured me that there *was* enough oxygen in my body; if there wasn't, I'd have already been dead hours ago. That information instantly did something to me, and I felt a lot better. Second, it explained that the problem was not the inability to take a deep breath but rather not exhaling properly. When we're desperately gasping for air without previously emptying our lungs, the lungs are still too full, and therefore there's no space for the new air to come in. I didn't even know if any of this information was true or not and whether there was any science behind it, but as soon as I read this, it was almost like my brain said, *Ah cool, it's all good then,* and I took one of those deep and crazy satisfying breaths. I exhaled slowly and thoroughly (without pushing it too far) and then took another deep breath in. Not every breath felt easy, but each time there was tightness in my chest, I knew it was nothing bad; I knew I wasn't in any danger, and despite the discomfort, the oxygen was still flowing in and that eventually, a nice satisfying breath would come.

What astounded me was how quickly I went from gasping for air, literally feeling like I was going to die, to being completely fine and able to breathe normally, just by reading a random piece of information on the internet from a questionable source. This was absolutely bonkers, and I started to wonder: If my mind can do this, what else can it do?

Finding a Breakthrough

This event triggered a significant and lasting change in me. All this time, I'd been letting my unchecked chaotic thoughts do whatever they wanted. What if there were things I could do intentionally, in a structured and organised way, to make my mind work for me all the time instead of just sporadically or by accident?

As with anything, to get better and make lasting lifestyle changes, you actually have to want it, and this was the breakthrough moment I needed. I literally couldn't wait to find out what I could achieve when I put my mind to it. When I was a teenager, I read *The Power of Your Subconscious Mind* by Joseph Murphy and thought I'd magically get fixed. I'd close my eyes once, force myself to visualise something I deep down didn't believe could happen, and then declare that the whole mindset thing was BS. It was, of course, a very superficial effort, and I simply wasn't ready or receptive enough to make lasting changes. It took me about twenty years to get there, but boy, was I ready!

As you already know, I had anxiety to deal with and a lot of mental clutter in my head, but it wasn't the only thing that was bothering me. It was also that nagging feeling that there was more to life than what society tells us to do. (You know: *be a good girl, go to school, get a job and then retire when you're too old and tired to actually enjoy what's left of your life.*) That I wasn't fully utilising my gifts, skills and experiences. That there was a real tangible value, I could add somewhere. That I could be more fulfilled and do something driven by real passion. I'd already sampled that passion during my dancing days, so I knew it existed and refused to believe that it was a one-off thing. I craved to feel it again. All these things had been bubbling under the surface for a while, but I kept ignoring them because my little rational brain just couldn't figure out what to do with it all. The day of my panic attack was the day I finally surrendered and made a promise to myself to be more open-minded and let myself just go with the flow. I have always been a 'logical' person, not interested in all that spiritual stuff, and didn't quite believe that we could somehow create our own reality with just our minds, which many of these philosophies teach. Educating myself on these topics was the start of a huge lifestyle shift.

Your Thoughts Create Your Reality

Your thoughts form your beliefs, and even more importantly, invoke feelings. The feelings you consistently experience shift you toward events and opportunities you want to attract into your life. At first, I struggled to get on board with the idea that your thoughts can literally create your reality and that you can somehow magically attract events into your life out of nothing. But if you think about it, on some level, we've all done it. For example, have you ever thought of someone you haven't spoken to for a long time and out of nowhere, this person suddenly calls or messages you? Coincidence, right? Another one of those coincidences happened just yesterday when I had lunch in a local restaurant. The waitress serving me told me that it was her first day, and she was terrified to drop a plate. I thought it was rather dramatic because the place was very quiet (almost empty), and she could take her time. She also had a sturdy tray that could comfortably fit a couple of plates. But five minutes later, I heard plates smashing, and two rather sizeable lunches ended up on the floor.

These are just small examples from everyday life that perhaps don't mean much. Still, having attracted big changes and opportunities into my life, I truly experienced this concept in action; I'll talk more about it later. The point is, I encourage you to fully embrace it and believe that it's incredibly important to pay attention to how your thoughts make you feel. They should make you feel good. Hence, I've dedicated the following chapter to the techniques that truly worked wonders for me and which I hope will help you use the power of thoughts deliberately.

There is a lot of information available, which can sometimes get overwhelming. Still, the approaches I'm about to describe are the ones that completely transformed the way I think and helped me declutter and organise my thoughts, leading to a happier, calmer and more fulfilled life.

Chapter 9

Taking Action on Your Mental Clutter

By now, you should have a list of your own personal mental clutter - thoughts, beliefs and behaviours that are not working in your best interest. All of these things are just little programmes that you repeat to yourself so many times that they become autopilot. So what's the best way to change them? Start consciously feeding your mind the thoughts you actually *want* to think. Why? As Steve Hightower – a janitor turned oil tycoon – said when asked if he had ever imagined he'd be where he is today: 'Absolutely. Because if you don't think that you can be great, you'll never be great. And I knew that I was gonna be great a long, long time ago.' So the underlying principle here is:

Your thoughts matter, and it's time to get them to work for *you instead of against *you.**

Replacing Negative Thoughts

Even though it might be hard to believe, thoughts are a *choice*. You can practise new thoughts the same way you practise a new yoga move. You're unlikely to walk into an advanced yoga class with no prior experience and hop straight into a one-legged crow pose. You'll probably not see a drastic change in how you think after a week or two of doing this work, so don't obsess about the outcome and just go with it. Be persistent and have fun. Personally, it took me six to eight months of small daily efforts to wake up one day and realise, 'Oh shit, I think *so* differently compared to a year ago! I can't believe that I used to stress about such ridiculous things!' It will feel awkward initially but suspend your disbelief for now. Become an observer of your thoughts, and when you notice a limiting one, consciously choose one that feels better. Over time, the small incremental improvements add up, and you'll be surprised how far you've come.

Below are a few examples of reframed thoughts.

Old Thought	New Thought
I hate uncertainty. I just want to know what's ahead of me. I hate nasty surprises.	I actually think that uncertainty is fun. Imagine having no surprises in life ever again, living a scripted life and knowing what will happen for the rest of my life. . . . HOW BORING WOULD THAT BE? Uncertainty is what keeps things exciting. When I feel uncomfortable, I know that I'm

	getting out of my comfort zone and growing in the right direction!
I don't like that friend; I feel like she always judges me. But if I drop her, who else will I go out with on Fridays?	I'd much rather spend a lovely evening alone (great company!) and read a good book/watch a great movie than be someone's doormat.
My parents were disorganised. It's probably in my genes too, so I'm going to be messy forever.	I am not my parents, and I make my own decisions. Organisation is a skill, which means it can be learned. Therefore, I take small and consistent actions and become better at them daily.
I wish I was more confident.	I don't wait until I know something perfectly before feeling confident because perfection doesn't exist. What I have confidence in is *my ability to learn*. I can fully learn how to be better at [*insert activity*]. Plus, confidence breeds confidence; when I feel confident, people perceive me as confident, making me feel even more confident.
I hate confrontation.	I have healthy boundaries, regardless of who I disagree with. When I need to confront someone who intimidates me, I ask myself: *How would I respond, and what would I say if that person was my good friend/someone I feel comfortable with?* My opinions are

	as valid as those of other people, so I assertively express them. Also, I deserve to be happy. If someone hurts me, I tell them. They are not mind-readers, and they may not even know that they upset me!
I am shit at my job.	I am badass at my job, and I'm continuously learning to be even better. Nobody knows everything, even the most experienced people. Even they don't get a printed step-by-step formula on what to do and have to learn as they go along.
I hate presenting, and I suck at it.	I'm a confident presenter and communicator because I have valuable things to say. The presentation is just an update. I simply tell people about the work that I've done. If someone asks a question and I don't know the answer, I say so and get back to them once I've found out. That's completely normal, and nobody knows everything. Also, nobody is actually focusing on *me*. People are interested in the content, not me, so there's no point stressing about being judged.
I've had anxiety since I was a child, so there's nothing I can do about it.	I've *experienced* anxiety, but that's not who I *am*. There is always something I can do. To start with, I commit to daily mindset work, even if it's just ten minutes a day. I

	acknowledge that I wouldn't be human if I didn't worry from time to time - everyone does. But I can choose whether I indulge in it and let the worry completely take over or swiftly move on. It's also completely normal to feel fear when doing something new. I feel the fear, but I go after my dreams anyway like a bulldozer because worries and fear don't rule my life!
What if I never find passion in life/don't have enough in my retirement fund, and end up homeless/get cancer/get hit by a bus/a person I care about gets sick?	'There is no situation that isn't made worse by worry. Worry never solves anything. Worry never prevents anything. Worry never heals anything. Worry serves only one purpose: it makes matters worse.' - Bob Proctor[7]
I'm stuck. My life is shit right now, and there's nothing I can do to change it.	Anybody can do well when things are going their way. But I also choose to do well when things are seemingly shit. I'm the creator of my life, not a manager of my circumstances anymore. There is always something I can do - even when the situation is seemingly hopeless. It's just a matter of training my brain.
I can't simply stop negative thoughts . . . it's impossible. They just keep coming.	Negative thoughts are a habit. And I can change it in the same way it was created - through the repetition of information.

	Therefore, I am consciously choosing new beliefs that support the habits I want to develop and then planting them in the place of the old beliefs in my subconscious mind.
I can only count on myself. If I was in trouble, there would be nobody to help me.	I have an amazing support system and feel safe because my friends are there for me. The right people gravitate toward me. I trust that help will appear when I need it, at exactly the right time.
What if people think I'm stupid?	I acknowledge that I won't please everybody, but that's fine. I care about what I think about myself and not what other people think of me. I recognise that to be truly happy, I can't be emotionally dependent on other people and addicted to what they think of me!

Make sure that the new thoughts *feel* good. If you're really struggling to get behind a new thought and mainly feeling doubt or resentment, there are two things you can do.

1. Debunk the thought

Find **evidence** that your current belief is not 100 per cent true. Let's say you have quite a lot of excess weight, but you're currently in the mindset of *I'll forever be fat/it's impossible to lose this much weight/my metabolism is just* *too slow.* Do some digging and find examples of people in a similar situation that have successfully lost weight healthily and sustainably. People who, instead of following fad diets, made small, gradual, lasting changes to their lifestyles.

If you're struggling with your weight, look up Marvin Ambrosious. He is a perfect example of someone who used to be overweight but decided to turn his life around and make healthier choices when it comes to food and exercise. But he didn't stop just there. He fell in love with the process so much that he became a personal trainer (a *really* good one as well . . . not one of those cookie-cutter PTs that give the same template workout plan to everyone and permanently look bored, but one that can offer anything from an easy five-minute workout to get you moving to a badass callisthenics session that will leave you pooped for days, depending on your specific fitness level and needs). Over time, he built an incredible career doing many really cool fitness-related things, including his own TV programme. So there you go; you now have proof that it's possible to become healthier, get the body you want and even enjoy the process. Here on Earth, someone's done it already and there's evidence against your limiting belief.

You might think you're 'not destined to have money' because 'your family didn't have much' or 'you're just not that kind of person'. Andres Pira, an author of one of my favourite books about mindset, called *Homeless to Billionaire: The 18 Principles of Wealth Attraction and Creating Unlimited Opportunity*,[8] is the perfect example of these statements simply not being 100 per cent true.

Andres wasn't born into a wealthy family. As a teenager, he acted up, partied heavily, dropped out of school, overindulged in alcohol and eventually became homeless. After a friend gave him a mindset book to help with his stinky attitude, he thought it was ridiculous but tried the techniques anyway, just to prove that they didn't work and because he had nothing better to do. To his surprise, it did work, he's now an incredibly successful real estate tycoon, and his message is: 'I'm a high school dropout who's been homeless, bankrupt and clinically depressed. If I can change my fortune, anyone can.'

2. Get on the thought ladder

The second thing you can do if you're struggling to get behind a new thought is to **upgrade it gradually**. Think of it as a 'thought ladder'. If you currently see yourself as not confident at all, there's a high chance that simply repeating 'I am confident' might not resonate with you immediately. Consider this thought progression:

I completely lack confidence -> It's possible to become more confident -> I am in the process of becoming more confident -> I am a confident badass.

There could, of course, be more progressions in between – you just have to find what resonates with you in this specific moment in time. It can always be upgraded later once the thought you've picked has become your new norm. Remember:

When it comes to mindset, it's not all black or white. There's plenty of grey in between, and grey is great! Use it to your advantage.

Similarly, if you're currently earning £20k a year and have a mountain of debt and would love to become financially secure, saying 'I'm a millionaire' might feel like a completely abstract concept. It might feel great, in which case stick with it! But if it doesn't, what's the number that *feels good* to you? Something that feels like a stretch from where you are now, but not impossible? Something achievable that feels right for you: £40k? £60k? £100k? You might not know at this point *how* you're going to get there. You just have to tune into your intuition and pick a number you can get behind.

Don't feel like you have to adhere to strict rules to get this process to work for you. That just kills the fun and excitement of it. There's a lot of information saying you *have to* say affirmations 100 times a day every day (yes, 100). You *have to* meditate every day. You *have to* set deadlines for your goals, or you *have to* handwrite in your journal because typing on a computer is less effective. And that's cool if it resonates with you. My thoughts? *Fuck. That.* Nothing that feels forced will give you the results you want, so you have to create your own unique routine that you truly look forward to.

I like to sit down every morning with a bucket of coffee and read the whole list of my new, reframed thoughts out loud. It helps me get into the right mindset to go about my day and feel excited about my morning. Forcing myself to repeat endless affirmations creates resistance and actually disengages my brain. I'd rather say it to myself once and *really feel it* instead of 100 times and feel nothing. The key is to do them regularly because, at the end of the day, you're working on developing new habits. But it's much more effective to do something for twenty minutes a day, five or six times a week, than hammer it mindlessly.

On top of that, I despise handwriting and forcing myself to do it results in me skipping important thoughts and reflections altogether, just because I can't be arsed to write. So handwriting may, in theory, be more effective – but not if you're going to cut corners! Typing, on the other hand – that, I thoroughly enjoy. Having had two very different university experiences – one in Poland where lecture notes had to be handwritten versus England where notes were printed out or typed – I can confirm that I saved a crap ton of time and learned more when I didn't have to handwrite. Even though scientific studies confirm that handwriting is more effective than typing, and therefore, I'm likely an anomaly in this scenario, it highlights that there's no one correct approach. You should do what *feels* good for you.

Meditating in a rush or when I'm exhausted and about to fall asleep is also not something I've ever benefited from. Finally, giving myself a deadline to hit a goal – whether financial or something softer, like becoming more confident – only adds more pressure, making me doubt that I'll achieve my goal in time.

Action

Go over your negative thoughts, beliefs and behaviours and rewrite them. Change the story you tell yourself and start repeating it to yourself regularly. Find five or ten minutes a day to read the list of your new and improved thoughts out loud. Really feel how good the new thought feels. When a negative thought pops up as you go about your day, consciously reframe it there and then.

Negativity Detox

Becoming aware of how many irrational thoughts roamed free in my head but weren't backed up by any real evidence actually blew my mind. Being a very logical person, I almost felt offended seeing all this mental 'clutter' written down in a Word document, staring back at me. That's why reframing all those ridiculous thoughts was a hugely satisfying and enjoyable exercise. However, you'll be fighting an uphill battle if the environment around you is filled with negativity that counteracts your efforts.

After practising noticing my negative thoughts and doing the thought reframing work for some time, I realised that things started to change. I became hyperaware of not just my mental clutter but also other people's. Previously, I rarely registered these things. Now, they were everywhere. The false impression given by the news telling us there's very little good out there. People in unhappy marriages or relationships pretending that everything is okay and sacrificing their happiness because it is easier that way and better than being alone. People endlessly complaining about their jobs (one person I know complained about their circumstances for over *ten years* but never did anything to change it). Not long ago, I'd just nod and agree that 'things were bad'. But now, my default had changed to 'So what are you going to do about it?' Now I know there are always options, even though they may not be immediately obvious.

Not all of these things are bad, and I'm not saying you shouldn't support a friend or relative going through a bit of a rough patch and needs to talk to get it out of their system. However, there is a lot of pointless negativity around us, which can easily jeopardise the progress we make. It's a lot harder to work on yourself when negativity comes at you from every direction like a ton of bricks. Fortunately, you can do things to tune it out and stop giving it your attention.

One of my absolute favourite and highly effective mindset experiments was detoxing from unnecessary negativity around me. This is particularly important when you're in the early stages of your mindset work because shielding yourself from negative influences will be like creating a protective bubble around yourself – an incubator for the new you, where you have the space to grow and explore what works and what doesn't. Here are the things I did to create that protective bubble:

Goodbye Google Discover

I disabled the news on Google front page. Google has a 'Discover' feature that shows you headlines for selected news articles and other pieces of content as soon as you load the search engine on your mobile. These headlines were often truly horrific, describing horrible crimes or traumatic events. Although my resting bitch face might say otherwise, deep down, I'm a very sensitive person, and information like this tends to stay on my mind for a long time. There are things I saw on TV as a child which I still remember now. *Do I need it in my life? No.* Other things that I 'discovered' were simply contradicting or annoying: '30 minutes of exercise a day will make you healthy' and '30 minutes of exercise a day is not enough to make you healthy'. Sigh. So Google Discover had to go. Bye, bitch.

Social media declutter

I unfollowed people on social media. I am not interested in seeing airbrushed abs and people pretending their lives are perfect. Don't get me wrong, I still follow some insanely fit people, but the ones that actually share interesting and useful content about nutrition, fitness and lifestyle, showing the good, the bad and the ugly. Powerlifters, nutritional experts, contortion and flexibility coaches, Ninja Warrior contestants or those who share helpful callisthenics tips. These people inspire me and add value to my life. I also stopped following accounts that spam me with messages I'm simply not interested in. People moan about their lives just to get some attention or share things that simply don't resonate with me or even annoy me. One of my ex-colleagues at one point became an avid supporter of Nigel Farage, and my feed was literally being filled with constant vomit of UKIP propaganda. Unfollowed.

I also stopped watching the news. Same reasons as

above. Every now and then, I'll do a quick scan of the main headlines just to know what's going on, but I don't need to fill my head with lengthy, elaborate and gloomy discussions.

Adieu notifications

I disabled Twitter notifications. I like Twitter, and I think it's great for finding specific discussions. However, I don't need the constant push notifications popping up on my phone, telling me how many people have died in car accidents or stabbings, what crazy shit such and such a politician has done this time or that there's a third world war happening as we speak, so we're basically all fucked. If there's a topic I want to read about, I find relevant discussions myself.

Cut ties

I stopped putting effort into one-sided relationships. There were people in my life who clearly valued my friendship less than I valued theirs. At one point, I'd bent over backwards to please them, help them when they were in trouble, and always be the one showing initiative to meet up or even keep in touch over the phone. But they weren't doing any of this for me. I don't keep scores with my friends; you just know when the relationship is balanced because it feels right. Sometimes I give, sometimes you give. But when one person always gives and the other takes, you find yourself in an imbalance that often causes stress and heartache. So I decided that I deserved better and cut ties with people who didn't put effort into the relationship.

Be aware of sharing

I stopped telling people about my plans or ideas if I knew they would be unsupportive. Even though their opinions are just that - *opinions* - they can really bring us down at times and leave us feeling deflated. Not what you need when you're in the middle of a major mindset upgrade! I learnt it the hard way when I made the mistake of telling my relatives that I was interviewing for a new job in the middle of the pandemic.

At that point, I'd done a lot of mindset work to get myself to a place where I was genuinely excited about the unknown, open to new opportunities and a lot more comfortable with risk-taking. I was proud of myself and the progress I had made. Also, this was a very early stage of the interview, so I hadn't even made up my mind whether I wanted the job or not. I hadn't even been offered the damn role yet! I intended to interview the hiring company as much as they interviewed me. The last thing I wanted was to end up in a job I'd hate, so at that point, I was completely detached from the outcome and focused on gathering as much information as possible and determining whether they were a good fit for me.

My relatives, however, went straight into the 'what-if' mode, focusing on all the worst things that could happen. 'Is this really the best time to change jobs? Can't you wait until the pandemic is over? Surely this is quite risky. You'd need to go through a probation period. What if you end up with no job?' The list goes on. Now, I know that their intentions were far from malicious. They love me and want the best for me. But the worries they were expressing and things they were saying actually made me really sad and left me with that dreaded heaviness in my chest.

I'm a big girl, and I'd done my risk assessment, so I didn't tell them about the interview to get advice. I told them because I was excited and wanted them to be excited too. To trust my judgement, be happy for me and tell me how proud they were. But I realised that I could say these things to myself, but I couldn't expect others to mentally be where I was. I'd done a lot of mindset work; they hadn't. I changed the way I see things; they hadn't. And that's okay. I can't control other people, but I can control what I say. I also became more selective about who I talk to about things that really matter to me to protect that new mindset I spent so much time building. And I sure as hell no longer take advice from people who never achieved the thing I'm trying to achieve! This might sound selfish, but it's not. Your happiness is something *you* need to go after; others can't do that for you. And deep down, you know what you need to tune out of and what you need to keep to yourself for that blissful peace of mind.

Stop verbalising negativity

I stopped talking about negative things all the time. There's power in verbalising your thoughts. Let's say you had to sit in a boringly irrelevant meeting for an hour, and it pissed you off. You have two choices.

One: you can think about what happened, reframe it, decide that it was unimportant in the grand scheme of things and think about what you've learnt (for example, you could decline similar meetings in future).

Two: you could bitch about it to all of your besties, repeating the same story from the beginning to each one of them, going over the annoying details and therefore marinading in anger that could have dissipated a long time ago. Trust me, I've done it plenty of times. And I noticed that each time I felt exhausted. Going over the event that upset you multiple times drains your energy because, emotionally, you're putting yourself through it repeatedly. And your friends and colleagues often encourage overindulgence in shitty thoughts by being overly sympathetic and telling you how unfair life is on you.

Moral of the story: verbalising negativity perpetuates it. I'm not saying to never get anything off your chest ever again. It's actually healthy to do so, but be intentional about how you deal with it and don't overindulge. Instead of bitching and moaning, your goal should be to see the situation from a different perspective, start feeling better about it as soon as possible and move on. And choose the person you talk to about it wisely - someone who will listen and then put you back in your place without babysitting.

The kind of negativity cleansing I outlined above can be hugely effective, just like getting rid of clutter from your home and throwing away things that are broken or not serving you anymore. Peeling off negativity from your environment will have a calming yet refreshingly energising effect on you.

Action

Spend some time thinking about and noting areas where you experience negativity and ways to tune out of it.

Surrounding Yourself with Positive Messages

If you think of your mind as a drawer full of old and unwanted crap, imagine that it's now been cleared and is ready to be carefully and intentionally filled with things that you're going to love and appreciate for years to come. It's a very special drawer where you'll keep your most important valuables – not disposable fashion socks you accidentally picked up whilst aimlessly wandering around Primark.

So what did I do to fill up my shiny new squeaky clean 'drawer'? I started consuming content that told me that I *could*. I went out there and literally inhaled every bit of content that had the potential to support me on my quest to become the person I wanted to be. I found books, blog posts, TV programmes, YouTube videos, Instagram accounts and podcasts on the topics of spirituality, manifestation, money mindset, shadow work, intuition, life purpose, career alignment, self-discovery, motivation, witchcraft (yes, really), Human Design, breathwork, entrepreneurship, empowerment, Qi Gong, sigil magick, Mercury retrogrades, energy healing, tapping, Law of Attraction, mindfulness, hypnotherapy, creativity, meditation, confidence, theta healing, subconscious mind, conquering fears, Tarot (which, contrary to common beliefs, is not going to magically tell you your future, but rather is a tool to tune into your intuition) and also interviews with inspiring guests.

Many of these things resonated with me; others didn't. But the point was, I learned something from each one of them, even if I didn't end up adding it to my routine. On top of that, all these messages were positive and empowering, and that's exactly what I needed. Bear in mind that if your life has so far been filled with negativity and you've developed certain thinking patterns, you won't undo it by reading one Instagram post. So I made a conscious decision to tune in to uplifting, empowering, and educational messages as much throughout the day as I possibly could.

I'd wake up in the morning and go over my affirmations and reframed thoughts to start my day like a champ. I'd then read a little bit of a chosen book before starting work. Even if it's just one or two pages, it all adds up and makes a big difference. Lunch breaks and evenings also provided a great opportunity to read something uplifting. When it wasn't practical to read, because let's say I was cleaning my flat, doing laundry or putting my makeup on, I'd always listen to a podcast.

I remember picking up Saturn, one of my guinea pigs, from a rescue centre and bringing her home. She was absolutely petrified and spent a few days hiding in a tunnel. Each day, I'd sit in the same room with her and talk so that she could get used to me and my voice. She'd never take food from my hand, but I kept trying every day. Eventually, she ate from my hand, then she started hopping on my lap when there was food, then she let me catch her without running away. Eventually, she relaxed and trusted me enough to have a cuddle and a nap on my lap.

Your mind is a rescue guinea pig. Just like Saturn slowly learning to trust me, with time and repetition, my mind began to accept the new messages as true, and my default thoughts started to change. None of this happened overnight, but who cares; I enjoyed the process so much, and I still dedicate time to discovering new content every day. I encourage you to give it a go. Suspend judgement and disbelief for a bit, and just explore the concepts you may be currently dismissing. You won't know if something resonates with you until you try it. You're not losing anything by venturing out and trying new things, and you can *always* go back to your old ways.

Why is it so important to go out there and look for new content? Because you, my friend, are stuck in one perspective - yours. And if you really want to change, you're going to have to broaden your horizons and see things from many different angles before you find what works for you.

Even if a particular concept or a person doesn't resonate with you, it's incredibly exciting to just *explore*! I see it almost like a treasure hunt. What new and inspiring concept/story/person will I discover today? And the beauty of this process is that most of these finds are almost always going to lead you to something else, so the growth and exploration never need to end!

On top of swapping negative influences for the empowering ones, it's also incredibly important that the physical environment around you encourages positivity and makes you feel good. This is why Part I of this book is entirely dedicated to transforming the space around you into your sacred place. So if you still haven't dealt with your physical clutter, now would be the perfect time to do it!

Action

Find at least a couple of new sources that promote positivity and tune into them daily, as often as you can. To get you started, I've put together a list of my personal favourites, which you can download for free from my website: www.dominikachoroszko.com/free.

Making Loving Decisions

The way you make decisions can tell you a lot about yourself. It can provide insight into mental clutter you didn't know you even had! A great exercise, which ties into the self-awareness piece from earlier, is to observe the motivations behind your decisions. It could be a decision to do something, to pursue a desire or even to remain in your current circumstances.

Anytime you make a decision, big or small, ask yourself: Is it out of love? Or out of fear?

Anyone who knows me is aware of how much I love fitness. I always have a fitness-related 'project' I'm working on. Back in the day, I got into bodybuilding, then callisthenics and then contortion. But all of these activities were always accompanied by the feeling of immense pressure and stress. I'd often say, 'I *have to* train today' or be deeply upset and beat myself up if I wasn't yet strong or flexible enough to perform a specific move. Why? Because I was doing it for the wrong reasons. I wasn't enjoying the journey. I just wanted to get to the final outcome. Why? Because for the longest of time, I felt worthless without dancing. *Boom.*

The fear of being worthless, unless I prove myself somehow, wasn't something that ever remotely entered my conscious mind until I started digging deep into my motivations. That realisation was truly a breakthrough moment. I mean, how the fuck was I meant to feel calm and happy when I was constantly forcing myself to do something that caused me stress and anxiety??

Does this mean that I completely stopped training? No, of course not. But now, I tune into my body instead of my ego and make decisions that support my wellbeing and happiness - from a place of love. I'm not a professional contortionist, nor do I want to be one, so I'm no longer forcing my body to endure positions it feels unhappy in. Instead, I practise maintaining a good level of flexibility because it makes me feel healthier. I feel happy and at peace with myself training because it brings me joy, not because I have to. You will, of course, have your own unique scenarios to work through, but here are a few common examples to get you started.

Decision/desire	Fear-based motivation	Love-based motivation
Buying an expensive designer handbag	It's a symbol of status, and I want to look like I'm rich. I want people to envy me. (Fear: feeling	I have admired this particular design for a long time and having it will bring me so much joy. Plus, I can now

	worse than other people.)	comfortably afford it, so it won't strain my finances.
Staying in a relationship	My partner and I haven't had sex in months, and we've grown apart, but that's what happens to everyone eventually, right? Plus, it's better than being alone. (Fear: loneliness; not believing that you can stand on your own feet.)	I feel so happy with my partner, and we have loads of fun together. I don't need them, but I'm choosing to be with this person because, even though I'm already content in my life, they bring in even more joy and happiness.
Holding on to belongings	Clutter makes me feel stressed and overwhelmed, but I can't really throw it away because there are so many memories in all of these items. Also, many were gifts, and it's rude to throw them away. (Fear: forgetting happy memories;	I surround myself with things that make me feel good. Every item in my home has a purpose and a place. I know how much physical possessions can affect my mental health, so I actively prioritise my wellbeing and only keep

	not wanting to be perceived as selfish and ungrateful.)	the things that serve me *today*. I know that loving myself doesn't mean that I don't love others; these are not mutually exclusive!
Buying a new car	All of my friends and colleagues are driving nice cars, so I should really upgrade mine. (Fear: feeling worse than other people.)	The new car will make me feel a lot safer and also, I love how comfortable it is!
Accepting a job offer	I hate my current job so much that I'll take anything just to get out of it. (Fear: not believing that the right opportunities exist; not believing you're worthy of the opportunities you truly want.)	I have accepted this job offer because it aligns with my career goals.

A decision in itself is not inherently good or bad, but what's important is to get to the bottom of what drives it – love or fear.

Action

Anytime you decide to pursue something you want or choose current circumstances, check with yourself: What is it that actually motivates you? Spend some time reflecting on your past decisions and ask yourself whether they were driven by love or fear.

Gratitude and Appreciation

As I said earlier in Chapter 9 (*see* Stop verbalising negativity), bitching and moaning only keeps you stuck in the negative energy. An amazing antidote is to focus your attention on the things in your life that you're grateful for and learn to appreciate the present moment.

How do you do that?

Start with a brain dump of everything that you're currently grateful for. Small, big, trivial, obvious, things you take for granted – everything. If in doubt, think how you'd feel if you *didn't* have that thing in your life. Aim to list about twenty or thirty things, but feel free to keep going until you can't think of anything else. Here is an extract from my personal list to give you a flavour of what I'm talking about.

Things I am grateful for:

- My partner.

- My friends and family.

- The money I'm earning now.

- Being able to walk.

- Being able to see, hear, smell and taste.

- Being organised.

- I have the heating on demand, hot water and electricity.

- I can speak two languages fluently.

- The apricot Danish from Marks & Spencer I'm eating right now (whoever came up with this thing needs to get a promotion).

- Being good at budgeting and managing my personal finances.

- My beautiful apartment.

- My investment portfolio growing over 40 per cent last year.

- My guinea pigs roaming around my flat.

- I eat delicious food every day without worrying about the cost.

- I am healthy.

- Being able to try new dishes from all over the world whenever I want to (in love with Fesenjan right now).

- Being financially independent.

- Having the freedom to do what I want.

- Having a good eye for interior design.

- My mechanic who does an amazing job looking after my car and is also a good friend.

- My strong body that supports me every single day.

- My sofa - literally the most comfortable thing ever.

- This delicious coffee in a beautiful copper cafetiere that I'm drinking now.

- How my mattress is so comfortable.

- My kitchen bin.

Really *feel* grateful for every item on your list, and don't be afraid to throw some self-love into the mix! You're not 'full of yourself' for appreciating who you are.

What do you do when you have the list? Feel free to come back to it whenever you want. You could either reread it fully or pick three or four items from that list every evening to end the day on a high. Alternatively, you could simply reflect on what you were grateful for that particular day before falling asleep.

Tip

The gratitude process doesn't have to be 'formal'. More often than not, I tend to just appreciate random moments as I go through my day: *Fuck, I love my apartment! This new throw is stunning and complements the wall art so beautifully! Oh my god, how delicious is this ice cream?!*

There is an interesting by-product of doing this work. When you practise gratitude and start appreciating the actual moment you're in, you silence all of your mental diarrhoea. All the worries, doubts or anxious thoughts disappear, and what happens, as a result, is that your creativity starts to blossom. From my experience, the creative flood gates most often open when I'm in a content state of just being, such as after meditation or when I go for a walk. Hell, I wrote a third of this book during my daily walks whilst admiring the trees, flowers, bumblebees and birds! Sometimes I had so many ideas coming at me out of nowhere that I'd come back home with a phone full of notes.

Action

Your turn now. What are you grateful for? Write down your gratitude list and read through it every day. Keep on adding things that you're grateful for or that make you happy that you're you.

Meditation

I have to make a confession. I used to *hate* meditation with a passion. First of all, I never really understood what it was and what exactly I was meant to be doing. Nothing about it sounded relaxing: sitting or lying down in an unnatural position, breathing in a way that's not comfortable and forcing yourself to stop the influx of thoughts. And of course, the harder you try, the more persistent and annoying the thoughts become. Even just thinking about the words I used just now to describe this process – forcing, unnatural, trying harder, annoying – causes my body to tense up! Which is the exact opposite of what you should be experiencing when you meditate. Fortunately, I'm stubborn as hell and kept researching and trying different approaches until I found one that worked.

In the end, what led me to find the 'winning' meditation approach was chronic lower back pain, which I suffered from for almost a decade. After hours of physiotherapy, needling, massages, trying many different stretching exercises, seeing a spinal surgeon, and having x-rays and MRI scans (according to which my back was completely fine), the pain was still there. And it was *bad*. I mean . . . how can the diagnosis be 'completely fine' when most days I struggled to get out of bed (I had to crawl out), couldn't lean forward to put my socks on, couldn't sneeze without pain and experienced spasms that had me falling on the floor?

So I started exploring the possibility of suffering from TMS – Tension Myositis Syndrome. According to Dr Sarno, the idea behind TMS is that the mind and the body are connected, and repressed emotions and anxiety can, in fact, cause pain in different parts of the body, but most notably in the back.[9] I could completely get on board with the idea of a mind/body connection. I mean, we've all experienced a headache or a stomachache as a result of stress or anxiety, so who's to say that it can't cause back, neck or wrist pain? What supposedly causes the pain is mild oxygen deprivation; long story short, you get stressed, your muscles tense up, blood flow to the muscles decreases, resulting in oxygen deprivation and discomfort in the affected area.

I'm not going to get into it too much, but the reason I'm mentioning this is that as I was researching TMS, I came across a very interesting concept[10] that I adapted and changed how I approach meditation. This method is particularly helpful when you feel anxious and want to calm yourself down.

1. Get in a comfortable position – this can be sitting or lying down, whatever feels best – and close your eyes.

2. Now focus on the bodily sensations caused by your anxiety.

3. Without judging the feeling as good or bad, think about where you're feeling it in the body. Is it in your stomach? Or perhaps your throat?

4. Then go deeper and, in your head, describe the sensations. Is it warm, cold, tingling, fluttery, intense, subtle, tight, sharp, racing, swirling? Inspect it with curiosity. And if unwanted thoughts come? Don't get stressed about it. Just realise that you've drifted somewhere else and bring your attention back to now. What you're basically doing here is being mindful. You're focusing on the present moment, not judging and simply being.

5. Stay here for a bit, maybe ten to fifteen minutes.

The beauty of this meditation is it quite literally dissolves the feeling of anxiety. Usually, when we feel anxious, we try to run away from this feeling because it's unpleasant. And does this usually work? No, not really. By avoiding it, you're reconfirming to your brain that it's something to be scared of, and in turn, it perpetuates the feeling of anxiety. By doing the opposite and focusing on the physical sensations caused by anxiety, you're signalling to your brain that it's okay – it's *not* dangerous. And . . . your brain loses interest.

This method works not only when you're anxious but when you simply want to go into deeper relaxation. In this case, when you close your eyes, simply scan your body for any tension. You might identify some tension, let's say, in your forehead; focus on it, give it your attention. As it slowly disappears, move your attention to another body part where you've noticed some tension and carry on with this scan for ten to fifteen minutes.

I love meditating when I'm starting to feel a bit overwhelmed. You know that feeling when you're working, your to-do list doesn't seem to be shrinking, and eventually, you feel like your brain is overheating? That's a great time to take ten minutes, step away from your desk, close your eyes and spend some time scanning your body for sensations. You will find that your brain cools down and begin to think more clearly again.

There is another benefit linked to regular meditation, which I mentioned before: with time, you become more intuitive, creative and more likely to come up with ideas. It doesn't necessarily happen during meditation – it can occur at a completely random point in time – but the point is good things happen when you start disconnecting from your mental clutter and practice just being.

Action

If you haven't tried meditating before, give it a test run. Try it for a week, ten to twenty minutes a day. Test out different scenarios, for example, when you're stressed or anxious and when you're not. Notice if the effects of meditation differ in any way when your mental starting point is different.

As you can see, there are many methods to choose from to tackle your mental clutter, so it's important to experiment and have fun with it. Don't try to cram everything into your routine all at once. These exercises are meant to help you feel calmer and more relaxed, so if you find yourself getting stressed, slow down and take your time.

Chapter 10

Dreaming Up Success

What do you do with that calming and breezy space in your home after throwing away all the crap that wore you down emotionally? You surround yourself only with the items and aesthetics that lift you up. And what do you do with all that 'delicious' space inside your head after you tamed the constant inflow of unhelpful thoughts? You fill it up with dreams. The less mental clutter there is, the easier it becomes to dream effectively. As Andreas Pira writes in his inspiration guide to creating abundance and wealth:

'Through visualization, we can alter the strength of our brainwaves to help us connect what we desire and our physical ability to achieve it.'[11]

When I decided to consciously start thinking more positively, I didn't know I was tapping into the idea that 'thoughts create reality'. I wasn't open to the 'spiritual mumbo jumbo bullshit' at the time, even though it was essentially that decision that got me out of the dumpster that my life was at the time. But one day, when I was ready and open to exploring previously dismissed concepts, I was journaling and had a realisation that quite literally blew my mind. In my journal, I was reflecting on my life and my achievements. It dawned on me that my thoughts had created my reality all along, without me even knowing it.

Before I get into the specific examples, I want to share Jim Carrey's quote, which in my opinion best summarises this idea of reality creation: 'As far as I can tell, it's just about letting the universe know what you want and then working toward it while letting go of how it comes to pass.'[12] There are essentially three parts to it:

1. Daydream.
2. Take action (I'll talk about it more in the next chapter).
3. Get out of your own way, and don't worry about how all of this will happen.

Therefore, your role in reality creation is to focus on points number one and two. Number three is not your job, so don't try to work out how this thing you want will happen because it usually happens in the least expected, random way. So just go with the flow. Otherwise, you'll drive yourself crazy.

Tip

Jim Carrey is not the only person who believes in the power of the mind. There are many others, including Will Smith, Oprah Winfrey, Jay Z, Steve Hightower, Andres Pira, Lady Gaga and Francis Ngannou. Seek out other inspirational people and stories to encourage you to do the mind taming work.

UFC fighter Francis Ngannou has one of the most extraordinary stories I've heard. He appeared on Joe Rogan's podcast talking about how he grew up in poverty in Cameroon, worked in sand mines from the age of ten, and how much he hated his life. Whilst digging in the sand, he'd daydream about what it would be like to be on an aeroplane, fly to America or France and have a better life. These visions pushed him to take risks and do things others weren't willing to do. He took a dangerous journey across continents with no money and even became homeless in Paris. Despite these adversities, he never stopped believing in his dream and eventually became a UFC heavyweight champion. I really encourage you to listen to the whole episode - 'JRE MMA Show #99 with Francis Ngannou'[13]. It's extremely powerful, and Francis goes into a lot of detail about what he's been through.

A really interesting thing he mentions is that most people he grew up with didn't have dreams. As long as they had something to eat, they didn't give a shit about making grand plans and thinking about where they'd like to be in a year or so. Francis, however, couldn't quite comprehend how people lived like that and saw a big difference between those who had dreams versus those who didn't. Twenty or so years have passed, and the latter are still exactly where they were before, whereas those who dreamt big grew steadily by consistently moving forward and taking one step at a time.

That's what visualisation is in a nutshell: daydreaming with childlike joy and excitement and the conviction that what we want is possible for us. A lot of New Age literature will have you believe that you have to set time aside, close your eyes, do some mandatory deep breathing and force yourself to think of your dream life in a minuscule level of detail. Frankly, I'm struggling to see Francis lying down with his eyes closed and performing visualisation rituals in the middle of a sand mine. And as I'm about to show you, this also wasn't the case for me. It's how strongly you *feel* about it that matters, not how or where you do it.

If you're one of those people who need juicy details and generic theories only prompt the question 'But *how*?!' (I'm one of them), below are examples of the things brought to life by daydreaming. If not, feel free to jump straight into Chapter 11, Getting Out of Your Head and Doing Something.

Moving to England

I explained at the beginning of Part II how much dancing meant to me and how fascinated I was by the dance teachers in England. Not only that, but I also dreamt of having ballroom dresses and shoes replaced more often. Dance shoes quickly get ugly from the constant use and heavy training, and I thought it was amazing when all of the top dancers changed their dresses a few times per competition. But both shoes and dresses were incredibly expensive, and my parents simply couldn't afford such luxury. To add to that, I daydreamed about travelling since I was a little kid, which was unrelated to dancing. And to quite specific locations: Japan, China, Hong Kong, Macau, Malaysia and Indonesia (Bali in particular). I could never have predicted that one phone call from a dance teacher I met once or twice would bring *all* of those dreams to life. I was invited to perform in all of those places, except for Bali.

And you know what happened? One of the competition organisers in Jakarta came up to us and asked if we'd like to 'pop into Bali' to relax after the competition, all expenses paid. You have to admit that it's a pretty big coincidence.

You might ask: 'Okay, so if daydreaming works so fantastically well, why did you end up hating dancing?' Well, to tell you the ugly truth, I never truly believed in myself as a dancer. I wanted it so badly, more than anything in the world. So badly that my insides hurt. But in my head, I never actually saw myself succeeding in the way I wanted. I never saw myself as a world champion. I saw obstacles: the money I didn't have, the other amazing dancers who I constantly compared myself to (and each time concluded that person X was better than me), the injustice in the industry and how you have to be pals with the judges to make it, the dance partner whose vision was the opposite of mine and many other roadblocks.

Even if these things were true, the right thing to do was to focus on what I *wanted*, not what was standing in my way, and work on erasing the word 'impossible' from my vocabulary.

Coffee shop job

I told you how at my rock-bottom I was running out of money but couldn't find a job. And then, out of nowhere, I felt the need to treat myself to a coffee. I followed that intuitive nudge, and by striking up a conversation with the barista who served me, with no expectations whatsoever, I got myself a job. And since my confidence level was at an all-time low, I got the kind of job I believed I could get at the time.

Romantic relationships

I haven't spoken much about relationships so far but let me tell you this: I used to be needy and desperate to be with someone. And nothing screams sexy like a needy and desperate girl, right? Why was that the case?

Well, for all the wrong reasons. I used to compare myself to others ('all my friends have someone and I have no one!'), and I viewed my current lack of a special someone as 'my fault' because, in my eyes, it meant something was wrong with *me*. Coincidentally, that was when I was somehow attracting the biggest trash of mankind. At one point, even I thought that it was impressive how they always gravitated toward me. It's like there was a secret noticeboard for shit guys out there, and someone posted my number on it! They were coming at me literally from every direction – control freaks, alcoholics, liars, cheaters, you name it. And each time, I'd see red flags but sweep them under the carpet because I thought that I was exaggerating, that I expected too much, that perfect relationships didn't exist and that I had to take what I could get and at least give it a chance. Self-worth and limiting beliefs were clearly a big problem for me, and I always prioritised what my boyfriends wanted over my own feelings. No wonder I was a magnet for pricks.

But then something happened that changed my life forever. I started dating a guy who was emotionally abusive and manipulative. And he'd do it in such a way that I didn't even realise I was being manipulated, which is quite freaky if you think about it. Deep down, I felt uneasy around him and had that weird feeling in my stomach, but again, I told myself that I was being dramatic. I remember lying in bed the day we eventually broke up and, for the first time in my life, feeling completely and fully at peace with myself. Calm. And that's when a thought hit me, and I've never been the same person since: *Why do I need to be in a relationship?'*

The thought wasn't bitter or negative; I was genuinely curious. In that one moment, I undid years of mental conditioning. I went against the cultural norm of having to be in a couple/be married/have children or else be called a 'spinster' and understood that there's a big difference between being with someone because they make you happy and being with someone because you are afraid to be alone.

I had freedom and independence. I could literally do whatever I wanted, go wherever I wanted and didn't have to explain myself to anyone. Why would I ever want to trade all of this to be with someone who makes me feel bad? Because if that's what a relationship is, then I don't want it! That was the night that I made a decision, and I felt very strongly about it: I was genuinely happy to remain single forever, and the only time I'd allow someone into my life was if that person *added* to it, without taking anything I already have away from me. And if I couldn't have it? Then I didn't want any of it because it was no longer necessary for me to be in a relationship.

Ironically, after blissfully enjoying my newly found freedom, walking around with a giant smile on my face and immersing myself in the new mindful way of life for about two months, I met someone. I remember feeling genuinely pissed off. I didn't want a relationship, but I felt weirdly drawn to him, and clearly, he felt the same. I liked him, but I liked myself more and wasn't ready to date just yet. So I decided there was no rush and took my sweet time to get to know him better – approximately four months. That's when we went on our first official date. It was effortless, and there was no pressure. We ended up being together for eight years, and it was the first 'normal' relationship I've had.

After so many years together, we eventually grew apart. Nothing bad happened. We simply evolved in very different ways and stopped making each other happy. Towards the end, we didn't have a single interest in common, different views on most things, the romantic spark was gone and we were pretty much just good housemates. Because nothing was majorly wrong and all of these changes happened slowly over time, it was very difficult to figure out why things felt a bit off. In the evenings, I'd often chill with a glass of prosecco and daydream about what I'd like our relationship to be: filled with constant fun and laughter, passionate conversation about anything and everything, encouragement to go after our dreams no matter how big or crazy, open-mindedness, spontaneity, adventure, willingness to try new things, deep friendship, and of course a romantic spark that could set the house on fire. These things were often at the back of my head, but because we kept drifting further apart, eventually, we broke up.

Little did I know that a person with all the missing qualities was already in my orbit. At the time, he was my best friend. And looking back, I met him around the time I started to feel unhappy and daydreaming about what I wanted. But I didn't see any of it, and the romantic spark wasn't there when we first met because I was simply not open to starting a new relationship; I was focused on fixing the existing one. It was only when I found myself single again (and happy to stay that way) that I realised that my romantic 'wish list' had come to life.

Some people might be quick to judge and say that getting into a new relationship so soon is just a rebound. Do what feels right for you because nobody can tell you that. Only you know your true motivations. And to me, it felt right to explore. Without pressure, without crazy commitments and with plenty of communication. The happiest relationships are formed from a place of freedom, joy and respect. People tend to get hung up on 'being together forever', finding 'the one', becoming 'official', the 'L word' and getting married. They force the relationship to 'work' to fit into their idea of perfection. That's pressure. And pressure kills the fun. So we built our relationship on the mutual understanding that over time, things might change. We might grow apart, we might meet other people who are more compatible with us or life circumstances might change, and that's okay. We don't want it to happen, but at the same time, we are detached from the outcome of staying together forever. What's fuelling the relationship is how much fun we have together *now*, in this present moment. Because the present moment is the only one that's real.

Relationships are probably one of the best examples of how my evolving thoughts and beliefs created several different realities. There was a direct correlation between the way I thought and the kind of relationships and people I attracted into my life. Anytime I experience doubt about the whole mindset thing, I remind myself of the power of thought and how it changed my relationships. And it's the slap in the face I need to return to a peaceful state filled with faith and possibilities.

Finding jobs

When I went back to university after quitting dancing, I was twenty-four. Most people would have already graduated, so as tempting as it was to pick a three-year degree and be done with it sooner (I really just wanted to go to work and get on with my shit), I decided that a more sensible option was to do a four-year sandwich degree with a year in an industrial placement. I knew I was a droplet in the sea of graduates all desperately looking for jobs, and the extra experience could give me a bit of a head start. What I didn't account for, though, was how hard it was going to be to find one of those elusive placements. *It. Was. Fucking. Hard.*

Completing long application forms, doing psychometric tests, phone interviews, and assessment days became my full-time job, on top of a full-time degree and twenty to thirty hours a week working at the coffee shop. I applied for over 100 positions, and let me tell you – these were all quality applications that took hours of research and pouring my heart and soul into it, not some half-arsed attempts written in ten minutes between lectures. Yet still, it took over nine months to finally secure a placement.

After graduation, I went through the same process to get onto a graduate scheme, but this time it took just over twenty attempts. I remember the moment I secured the position, and I thought to myself: *Wow . . . this is as hard as it's ever going to get when it comes to job hunting. In the future, there won't be this many people applying for the same job at the same time. It will literally be a breeze to find a job.'* And I was convinced that this was true. There was no shadow of a doubt. University lecturers kept scaring us, while news articles everywhere showed grim statistics of 400 applications per one graduate scheme.

In contrast, I couldn't imagine this being the case for a 'normal' job. In my head, there could be maybe twenty-five applications? Or maybe even five if the job was specialised in some way and not broadly advertised. Either way, I felt deep in my heart that it would be easy.

And a crazy thing had happened. All jobs that I ever had *were* easy to get. There came a time when I became unsatisfied with my job and decided to completely change my career path. I wasn't even sure if the role I wanted existed in real life, but I worked for a large company and thought I could just chat to a few people, ask around and see where it took me. Maybe someone could shed some light on other departments or point me in the right direction. What I did completely by accident was something that doesn't exist in an introvert's vocabulary – I networked. I met and spoke to *so* many people who did eventually lead me to a department that had my dream role. And . . . they were recruiting! It was a very niche department, and changes were extremely rare. So the fact that they had a new position that was opening was an absolute miracle. *What are the fucking chances?*

I met with the hiring manager a few times, and even though I didn't have much experience in that area, I already decided that I was getting this job no matter what.

I was determined and willing to learn. We scheduled an interview, and in the end, I was offered the job. The whole process felt effortless. All I did was talk to people, and that's how I got subsequent jobs too.

Finally, my favourite example: the job came to me. I remember very clearly sitting on my sofa, chilling with a glass of prosecco and thinking, *I'm a bit bored. I fancy a change.* None of this was serious, and I certainly wasn't in job-hunting mode. It was right in the middle of the pandemic, and everyone kept banging on about job losses and how fucked the economy was, so that didn't feel like the right time to go out there and conquer the world.

Nevertheless, I was simply thinking about the kind of job that hypothetically would make me happy. I thought of the role itself – team structure, salary, location, company culture, the kind of people I'd like to work with and what I'd like to learn. I thought to myself, *Hmm, wouldn't it be nice?* And carried on with my prosecco.

Two months later, I received a random email from an external recruiter. It was a Friday evening, and I was yet again chilling on my favourite sofa. When I read the email, I had this weird feeling in my stomach. I just *knew*. I somehow knew it wasn't happening by accident and that a big change was coming. I received these kinds of emails before, but this time it just felt different. So I scheduled a call with the recruiter. After speaking to him and doing some research on my own, my mind was blown because this job literally ticked every box on my wish list. It matched it so perfectly that I was borderline spooked. I obviously went ahead with it and just trusted that whatever was meant for me would come. And I got the job.

You can say that all of these examples were sheer luck. Funny, though, how luck seems to correlate with the shifts in mindset in any given area of life.

Pay rises

One of my biggest mental blocks ever was how much money I could earn. And let me tell you this: that number was low. Back in my coffee shop days, I thought £19k a year was a lot of money, and I struggled to picture myself earning 'this much', although overall, it felt somewhat achievable in the distant future. When I thought of £30k, though, I was genuinely convinced that this was beyond what was ever going to be possible for me in this lifetime. In my head, I kept questioning: *Who would pay me this much money and for what? I have nothing to offer that's worth this much.* Yes, my self-esteem was in the fucking basement. And even after I surpassed that 'unicorn' of a salary, each time I got another pay rise, I thought, *Okay, this is it, this is definitely my salary ceiling now.* And then something happened that would completely change how I thought about money.

It was during the time I networked my way to my dream job. There were many amazing and hard-working people there who took pride in their work. But there were also people who - let's not beat around the bush - were lazy as fuck. I saw them flipping between the same two spreadsheets to look busy, disappearing from their desks for hours, spending most of their time by the water cooler. When they eventually delivered some work, the quality was mediocre at best. When I found out that they were getting paid 35 per cent more than the people who actually worked hard, including me, I flipped. Not because I was jealous or comparing myself to others, but because I had finally gotten tired of my own shit and angry at my imposter syndrome. I thought, *Well if they can do this, I can too.*

My 'setpoint' had shifted, and I now genuinely believed that this amount of money was within my reach. I knew that I was good at my job, and now I also knew that someone who wasn't very good on paper was being rewarded more than me. I understood that a lot more goes into the number that's your salary than simply being a good girl who does what the boss says. Besides your work-related skills and the willingness to learn, you also need a sprinkling of belief in yourself and a dash of ruthless negotiation. So I decided to speak to my boss, and he agreed that I deserved a promotion. Fabulous. But if you ever worked in an office, you'll know there's usually a lot of corporate politics to overcome, and as such, months went by, and nothing had changed. So I decided to take matters into my own hands and promote myself. Coincidentally, a new opportunity for a more senior role became available. Of course, doubts crept in, but I quickly told myself to shut the hell up and at least apply. So I interviewed for the job, asked for a 35 per cent salary increase and ended up getting the job.

Companies are not known for rewarding employee loyalty, so a couple of years later, I found myself in a similar situation – unable to progress. But this time, I knew what to do. I applied for a new job and asked for a 30 per cent increase. At the end of the day, what's the worst that could happen? They could say no, in which case I would have kept looking until I found what I wanted. But they said yes.

My visualisations around promotions and pay rises were multifaceted because I do believe that once my mindset shifted and I had a new money 'setpoint', I attracted new opportunities. This was the element of 'magic' – the bit we don't really understand and where opportunities seemingly appear out of nowhere at exactly the right time. But the other side of the coin is that I also did something about it (I'll talk more about taking action in the next chapter). I went after what I wanted despite my doubts and worries, so now, the sky is the limit.

Guidance in life

It's easy to say visualise what you want, but what do you do when you *don't* know what you want? When you have that feeling deep in your heart that something is missing in your life, but you have no clue what that damn thing is? This was exactly where I found myself in 2020, and I had no idea where to even start searching, but the question was always at the back of my mind. And the answers came to me in the most unexpected ways.

When the pandemic fully kicked in and a lockdown was imposed, I had to tweak my fitness routine because all the gyms and fitness studios were shut. I thought it was the perfect time to start stretching more. I was relatively flexible and could do splits (with *many* warm-ups), but I always wanted to learn backbends and more advanced contortion poses. One day, I was faffing on my Instagram, and one of my uber flexible friends posted a story of her in a crazy pretzel-type pose and tagged her contortion coach, Athena. Even though I had no intention of working with a coach, I felt like checking who that Athena girl was. As I scrolled through her Instagram filled with pictures of poses humans should never be able to do, I found myself messaging her and asking for more details. I had no idea why, but I was insanely drawn to her. Like I had to have her in my life for whatever reason. A couple of days later, I did a crazy thing and purchased a full block of eight lessons. A sensible person would probably just start with one to see if it was a good fit, but I just knew I needed to do this.

Athena turned out to be an amazing coach and taught me a lot about my body, but more importantly, we became very good friends, and during one of the sessions, I confided in her that I was feeling a bit lost. Little did I know that she was really into the mindset work and would recommend many invaluable resources that shaped how I think today. And another interesting thing that came out of this experience was that even though I learnt some cool contortion stuff and got more flexible, seeing how much Athena enjoyed stretching made me realise how much I didn't. For her, it was her purpose and brought her joy. For me, it was ego-driven and a poor attempt to find a replacement for dancing.

This book

I told you earlier that for quite some time, I felt like something was missing in my life and that I wasn't utilising my skills and talents effectively. People often say that to figure out what you should be doing, you need to go back to your childhood years and reflect on the things you enjoyed doing. So I did. And as it turns out, it was a clusterfuck of random activities: I liked drawing, digging in the ground for hours to find fossils (I wanted to be a palaeontologist), writing poetry, dancing, collecting minerals, reading about geology, playing with Barbies and eating excessive amounts of mum's homemade cheesecake. Unfortunately, this exercise did jack shit in bringing me closer to my 'purpose'.

But I was fuelled by the success I had with 'accidental' visualisation and decided to try and do it intentionally this time. I started daydreaming and seeing myself fulfilled, happy, helping people, adding value and just enjoying doing whatever that 'thing' is.

Not long after that, things started to happen. Athena said to me one day: 'You should do an online course or something else to do with organising. You're so good at this! Oh, and look! I organised my drawers the same way you did. It's amazing! I can find everything, and it never gets messy!'

People started asking me how to redecorate their interiors and declutter their homes. Another friend told me how amazing I was at 'adulting' and how impressed she was that I managed to turn my finances around so drastically and learn to invest all by myself. I started to come across book recommendations that were dropping more and more clues to help me understand my values and personality; one of them, Ashley Stahl's You Turn,[14] helped me discover that I'm actually really into 'beauty' and 'words', aesthetics of all sorts, as well as reading and writing. At that point, I didn't really know what any of that meant and what to do with all that 'intel'. Until one day, I listened to a podcast. The host was talking about how combining all of the seemingly unrelated things that we enjoy doing is what makes us unique and how we can often find purpose when we combine them. And that's when it hit me: I love organising things around me. It makes me happy, calm and free. Doesn't matter *what* it is, but as soon as I organise it, I feel at peace.

It's often hard to see the things we're good at because they are so deeply ingrained in who we are. So it took time to realise that there were people out there who could benefit from my knowledge. Even if it's just *one* person. I felt that spark of excitement, and that's when I knew that I wanted to share this with people. I felt like I had a purpose!

Okay, cool. So how do I actually do that? Fortunately, I didn't have to wait long for the answer. Clues about writing a book were. Literally. Everywhere. People on random podcasts were giving advice on writing books. I started to come across books about writing and publishing your first book. I also had the sudden unexplained urge to buy a new laptop, even though the old one was rarely used. These things eventually led me to the realisation that deep down, I was dying to write a book. That state of Eureka was incredibly short-lived, though, because doubts and fear quickly crept in. 'Who am I to write a book? Who would even read this? Dominika, you dickhead, you're not a writer . . . stay in your lane.'

The thing about visualisation is that when you stick with it and keep daydreaming despite setbacks, the clues and hints are pretty damn persistent.

And the final clue came in the form of a . . . skin rash. A mysterious rash invited itself onto my face and refused to leave, so I booked a video call with a doctor who explained that skin conditions can often crop up as a result of stress and asked how things were going in my life. Although I wasn't sure where it came from, the flood gates opened, and I literally spewed on her how I hated my life, how it was lacking passion and how everything sucked and, holy shit, I went off on one. After all that verbal diarrhoea, I felt embarrassed and slightly guilty. I didn't hate my life, and not everything sucked. I was just frustrated and clearly needed to let off some steam. (Side note: I truly believe that it's better to let anger and frustrations out and be done with it instead of suppressing it.)

To my surprise, she didn't seem freaked out by my rant of the century. In fact, she revealed that she was a life coach, and we had a really productive chat. As you can imagine, my jaw was on the floor at that point. You have to admit: *What are the fucking chances?!* I learnt from my experiences that coincidences like this don't just happen for no reason, so after the call, I researched her online. She was indeed a very successful coach and . . . she had a book! Needless to say, I downloaded it immediately and inhaled the whole thing in one sitting. And . . . I hated it. Now, I don't mean it horribly at all. That person was clearly an amazing coach, and many people were recommending her book; it just didn't resonate with *me*. But something clicked in me, and I realised that just because I didn't like it, it didn't mean that others wouldn't find it helpful. We all have different tastes. And no matter what we say or do, there will always be critics out there who dislike it, and there will also be those who love it. That's just the way it is.

I thought to myself: *I could write a book and help people.* And then I heard a voice in my head saying: *So why don't you?* I kind of just sat there for a bit, and because I couldn't come up with a valid excuse, I started writing this book the same day. Having surrendered and put my doubts and worries aside, I poured my heart and soul onto every page of this book and found the joy, passion and fulfilment I was searching for.

Other thoughts on visualisation

I dedicated quite a lot of space to visualisation and went deeper into details because there are many misconceptions about it out there. Particularly in the spiritual community, where you can sometimes come across people who'll tell that all you have to do is just sit there, visualise, and you'll 'manifest' the things that you desire.

Yes, there is an element of 'magic' in the examples I gave you because I don't think science can explain why opportunities randomly start appearing when you focus on what you want and have more faith. I just know that there was a tangible difference between the outcomes I was getting when I was a miserable pessimist versus when I developed a brighter outlook on life. I couldn't argue with the evidence, so I decided to just accept it, despite my rational brain screeching and objecting to it strongly. However, you also need to take *action*. You can sit there and daydream until you're blue in the face, but things won't just appear in your life out of nowhere. Even to win a lottery, you need to buy a ticket first! The things that I wanted came to me eventually, some of them relatively quickly, whereas others took a long time and tiny, tiny, tiny, consistent steps toward my goals. It certainly wasn't instant. I'll explain what taking action may look like in the next chapter.

Action

Reflect on all the coincidences that led you to achieve the things you wanted and write them down. Do you remember how you felt about what you wanted before it became a reality? Can you backtrack to see how your thoughts created that reality? List as many of these coincidences as you can think of, both big and small, from as far back as you can remember. On top of that, make it a habit to daydream daily. It doesn't have to be 'formal', and you don't have to close your eyes or lie down. Just think of the things you want to achieve as you go about your day, and make sure that these thoughts *feel* pleasant.

Chapter 11

Getting Out of Your Head and Doing Something

It's pretty obvious that if you rot in bed all day and do jack shit, you won't magically wake up one morning to the life you want. You have to actually do something, and there are two parts to taking action, depending on whether you know what to do or whether you don't.

Part 1: Mindset Action

When we don't do what we want or go after our dreams, it is almost always down to mindset. We don't believe in ourselves. We worry that we will fail. And do you know what that is? Mental clutter. How often have you thought to yourself: *There are no good guys out there. I will never get a better job, so I'll just stick with my boring, low-paid one. I'm just bad with money. My metabolism is just very slow.* And all this mental clutter is literally stopping you from taking the first step toward the life you want because you're being discouraged by the possibility that you'll get your hopes up and then fail, despite putting all this time and effort in.

If you're in this stage, you may not know *precisely* what you want; you might be thinking that you'd like a new job, but you're not sure what it could be. Or maybe you're feeling uninspired and don't know what you should be doing in life. Because there are no concrete steps for you to take, you might be wondering: How the hell do I take action?

Action

This is the part where you focus on working on yourself, tackling your mental clutter and becoming better at tuning into your intuition. That's your action. This is where you clear out all the things that are no longer serving you and are standing between you and the life you want. The previous chapters were all about that. This is the stage where you *gain* more clarity and attract new opportunities.

Remember when I was completely broke and unemployed but decided to get out of my misery cave and treat myself to an overpriced coffee? Logically, it made no sense. But intuitively, I just felt like doing it; something pushed me to do it. And that coffee turned into a job offer which I so badly needed at the time.

I also briefly mentioned that when I was working in the coffee shop, I knew I needed to somehow get my shit together and started telling people (*anyone* who was vaguely willing to listen), 'I don't know what to do with my life.' This was my action. It might sound like nothing. How is that even an action? One of my regular customers had a director-level job in a big corporation. He was always friendly, and I really enjoyed chatting with him. One day, I shared my dilemma, and he said, 'There is so much you could do, you could even go back to university and learn what's out there. We could sit down together on a lunch break, and I could talk you through the process of applying if you want? Here, I'll give you my business card. Email me to find a suitable time.'

I met up with him, and he also brought one of his colleagues along. The advice they gave me was invaluable and helped me decide to go back to education. A couple of years later, when I was looking for industrial placements, he offered to help with my CV and ask if any placements were going at his company. It's incredible if you think about it: a random person offered to sacrifice his free time to help a stranger who served him coffee every day. I'll forever be grateful for his guidance.

How do you want to feel?

There is a helpful exercise you can do from time to time that requires writing down how you'd like to *feel*, who you'd like to *be and* what you'd like to *have*. The reason for it is that everything we want in life is usually not just for the sake of it, but because we crave to feel a certain way. By writing it all down, you get closer to your root motivations, and it becomes clearer what action you should take. And interestingly, there will be plenty of things you could do *now* to make you feel this way. Here's an example.

How do I want to *feel* (inner focus)?

- Excited
- Energised
- Free
- Fulfilled
- Grateful
- Comfortable
- Rested
- Generous

Who do I want to *be,* and what do I want to *have* (outer focus):

- I want to be a financially independent professional who doesn't rely on others for help with money.
- I want to live in a beautiful, trendy apartment.
- I want to have a personal trainer.
- I want to speak more confidently.
- I want to be more of a morning person.
- I want to drive a spacious car.
- I want to own property.

Keep writing until you can't think of anything else. This is a great way to start taking action because even though you might not be in a position to have everything you want right away, there's always something you could do to get you closer to each one of these things and make you feel the way you want to feel.

You can reflect on the things in your life that are currently making you feel excited and do more of them. Maybe eventually, this could become the source of your income?

You could go to sleep an hour earlier, take regular breaks throughout the day or meditate to feel more rested. What about being generous if you don't have much money? That's okay, too, as generosity doesn't have to involve money. It could be as small as helping a friend paint their kitchen, writing a positive review for a product you loved, ordering your takeaway from a small family-owned restaurant or donating items you don't use to a charity.

What about the second list with an outer focus? First, you could start by figuring out how to reduce your expenses and increase your income (we'll talk about it in Part III). You might not be able to move into a brand-new trendy apartment right now, but you could declutter your current place and style it with modern accessories. Hiring a personal trainer might not be a viable expense right now, but you could research free training programmes online or find free follow-along classes on YouTube. You could start waking up ten minutes earlier and increase that to twenty after a week or two to slowly build up a new habit. Your car might be small, but you could wash it, clear it out and treat it with the same respect as if it were your dream car. You might not have a huge deposit for a house. Still, you could buy a bunch of property books to educate yourself on different buying strategies, speak to a mortgage advisor or explore buying in a different area that might be cheaper.

Taking action can be the tiniest of steps, but it can lead to big things further down the line. Never underestimate the power of those little steps.

Part 2: Physical Action

This is where you have a concrete action to respond to a specific problem or opportunity. You may have been offered a job and now need to decide whether to take it or not. You might have an option to relocate to another city or country like I did when I was approached to represent England in ballroom dancing all these years ago. You may be unhappy in your relationship and facing some tough choices.

These things are a lot more specific than Part 1, and here is where you learn to embrace *change, uncertainty and risk*. And this may be challenging because, more often than not, it requires you to step outside of your comfort zone. So the key question is whether you're taking action out of love and inspiration or out of fear and despair - which we talked about in more detail in Chapter 9, Taking Action on Your Mental Clutter. Let's explore a few tips on taking physical action.

One step at a time

Marvel didn't start by planning out how to bring the whole interconnected universe onto the screen. They focused on the first film - *Iron Man*. The goal was to put all of their energy into it and make it the best movie possible. And once it proved to be a huge success, they took it from there. One movie at a time, individual characters were built, which culminated in them coming together.

We've been conditioned to plan out our entire lives. 'Pick a university degree that will start your career. Have a ten-year career plan. Find a partner for life.' The thing is, you will never be able to plan out your life because the future is unpredictable.

On top of that, we constantly grow and evolve. Our tastes and preferences change. We fall out of love. Just because you studied, accounting doesn't mean that you can't become a fashion designer if that becomes your passion later in life. And limiting yourself and forcing a certain lifestyle just because 'that's what you've planned' is one sure way to become miserable and feel trapped.

Attempting to figure everything out upfront is a huge task that can make you feel overwhelmed, frustrated and miserable, which in turn often causes paralysis by analysis; we end up doing nothing because the task ahead of us is so big that we don't deem it achievable.

Therefore, whatever action you have to take, take it *one step at a time*. Focus on the next step ahead of you and give it your full, undivided attention. And then see where it takes you. I think you'd agree that staring at a blank page, thinking 'I'm writing a whole book', can be rather daunting. But if you focus on writing one page at a time, it suddenly doesn't feel that bad. And if you complete one page a day, after a year, you'll have written a 365-page book. Small, consistent actions lead to a big result. So anytime you face a big task and start to feel overwhelmed, think: *Iron Man*.

Managing fear

I want to point out that taking action will most likely feel scary. It's scary to leave your comfort zone, especially when you're making big decisions and going through major life changes, but that simply means that you're venturing into the unknown. And the good bit is that the discomfort is only temporary, and we quickly get used to the new reality.

I used to be scared of driving. I mean it . . . I was *terrified* and had nightmares about crashing the car. It took me a very long time to pluck up the courage to even try it. But eventually, I thought, *Screw it*. I want the freedom that a car can give me, so I'm going to suck it up and just book my first lesson (*Iron Man, Iron Man, Iron Man*). And was it really that bad? In the beginning - yes. But one lesson at a time, I was slowly overcoming my fear, and because I didn't let it stop me, I now enjoy the freedom of hopping into my car whenever I want.

Remember that not taking action and staying in your comfort zone doesn't stop the changes from happening in the outside world! For example, you have no guarantee that staying in your current job is safer than going for that better job you actually want; you could be made redundant from your 'safe' job, and you'd have no control over that.

The fear is simply there to protect you, and it's in our nature to be wary of the unknown. But take my guinea pigs as an example. When I brought them home from the rescue, they hid in a tunnel for days, even though they had a giant two-floor cage, which was also opened during the day, so they could run around freely. It took a long time, but eventually, they started to explore. And now? Hell, now there's no stopping them! They're making full use of their penthouse, frolicking around the house whenever they feel like, doing 'zoomies' and just loving life. If they hadn't been brave enough to come out of the tunnel, they would have never experienced the freedom, fun and joy they have now.

Don't be a guinea pig stuck in a tunnel.
If your intuition tells you to go for it,
take action despite fear.

Final Words on Mental Clutter

Mental clutter is a real thing and should be dealt with in exactly the same way as physical clutter: you do an audit of the current situation to identify what you have, get rid of what you don't want, and finally, organise what's left by creating daily routines that support your goals. The techniques and strategies in Part II of this book should give you plenty of ideas to start experimenting and see what resonates with you.

Does addressing your mental clutter mean that you will never again experience anxiety, doubts or worry? No, of course not. These things will come, and that's completely natural. But decluttering your mindset will give you the tools you need to deal with them as and when they appear. Instead of giving in to them, you'll see them exactly for what they are - mental junk.

Part III

Grow Your Personal Finances

'Too many people spend money they haven't earned, to buy things they don't want, to impress people that they don't like.'

~Will Rogers

Chapter 12

Financial Carnage aka What Is Even Happening?

Money is one of those elusive things that's always surrounded by a crap ton of emotions and even more mental clutter. This is precisely why I wanted to tackle it *after* talking extensively about mindset. By now, you should be aware of any limiting beliefs or worries you may have around money and have hopefully started to reframe them already. But on top of that, you also need to actually *do* something to get on top of your financial shit – which is what Part III is all about. And before you roll your eyes, I promise you staying on top of your money can be easy and seamless (you won't ever need to put a block of time aside to 'manage your money', except for maybe one or two hours each year). And it's *fun*; otherwise, I wouldn't have stuck with it for over eight years! So stay with me.

When I first began working, my relationship with money was rocky, to put it mildly. To start with, there was not enough of it. But earning roughly £450 a month was relatively easy to manage because I couldn't really buy anything – £200 went on rent, and the remaining £250 was divided between food, bus tickets, toiletries and top-ups for my pay-as-you-go mobile phone.

My rent increased when I went back to studying and moved closer to university, so I cranked up the number of hours at the coffee shop, which bumped up my income to £750 a month. I still paid for rent, food, toiletries and bus tickets, and new expenses. I got myself a cheap contract on my phone, occasionally I'd buy some food from the university canteen, and I also had to buy textbooks. With so little money coming in, 'managing' my money never crossed my mind.

Somehow, I kept my head above water without ever going into overdraft, but there was a downside to this: my life was constantly filled with fear. Every time I had to spend money, I'd worry whether there would be enough in my bank account to cover it. There was no room for fun. Or even if there was, I wouldn't know anyway. I had no idea if I was saving anything from the previous month or if I had bitten into the 'buffer zone'. (My aim was to always have *some* money before each payday, even if it was just £10 or £20.)

In fact, money – or shall I say, the lack of – was such an enormous source of fear for me that even though I was given a maintenance grant from the government because of my extremely low income, I never actually spent it and saved it instead. Because, you know, what if I was suddenly to become homeless? At least I'd have something to keep me going for a while. So I decided that until I dropped dead from studying full-time and working almost full-time, I'd do whatever I could to cover all of my expenses from my income only and save the grant money for those times I was *really* desperate.

And do you know what happens when you live an

extremely restrictive lifestyle for a long time? Pretty much the same thing that happens after a prolonged diet of 800kcal a day and only eating cabbage soup and celery sticks – you go on the binge of the fucking century. So after I graduated, got a steady paycheck and smelt a bit more money, I literally couldn't stop myself from spending. What did I buy? Anything. Shitty disposable clothes, makeup, cheap shoes, handbags, body lotions.

Finding Freedom from Fear

Eventually, I started to get sick of accumulating high volumes of low-quality items, something that went against my values. They were taking a lot of valuable space (clutter!), and I wasn't in love with any of them. Plus, I also needed to somehow get out of that rut and start saving money. So I did something that will probably seem rather counterintuitive: I decided to make one last purchase and make it *big*. Something to reward myself for years of hardship and poverty. Something to conclude the era of spend-bingeing. Something that I'd actually love and cherish for many years to come. And since I'd been drooling over a very specific Mulberry handbag for a very long time (we're talking walking into the store just to smell the leather type of drooling), I decided that was going to be my 'thing'. Logically, it made no sense. But intuitively, I knew it needed to be done; it *felt* good. The question now was: *Where the fuck am I going to find a £1,000?* I had no idea what was going on in my bank account, where my money was going or how much I was even saving each month. And little did I know that the process of figuring out how to find the money for my dream bag was going to turn into a lifelong passion for money management.

Tracking my money not only meant that I was able to achieve my goal and get the bag in just two months but - similarly to when I properly decluttered my room for the very first time - I felt energised, happy and *really* in control of my finances. The fear and anxiety that hung above my head like a dark cloud every time money was involved were replaced by feelings of freedom and empowerment. And you know what the funny thing is? Seeing how fast I could save once I took control over my money made me want to spend less!

That was over eight years ago, and I've been on top of my financial shit ever since. Why? Because I made managing money quick and super easy! In the next chapter, I'm going to share with you exactly how to do this so that you can free yourself from financial chaos, organise your personal finances and start having fun with your money.

Chapter 13

Financial Awareness in a Nutshell

Only two factors affect your financial health: your *income* and your *expenses*. So to have more money, you need to:

*Earn more, spend less or a
combination of both.*

I know, I know - it's painfully obvious. And as much as I want there to be an exciting new 'recipe', there really isn't.

How can you increase your income? Firstly, don't fall for scams. Anyone that tells you that you'll be rolling in it in no time, with no effort and without spending any money upfront, is full of shit. 'Create a seven-figure business in thirty days, no need to do anything, just put your feet up and rest because my method will work for itself! Oh, yes, you have to pay £5k for my affiliate course, but it's an investment! It will basically pay for itself when you're a millionaire!'

No, no, no. The only person getting rich in this scenario is the affiliates/drop shipping/property 'guru', and sadly social media is *riddled* with stuff like this. Some of these scams are blatantly obvious, but others aren't. As someone keenly learning about property investment, I find myself questioning everything because it's hard to tell what's real and what's not when you're new to the subject.

To really answer this question, you have to dig deep within yourself because you're the only one that knows your unique skills, talents, interests and passions. There could be whole books written about this topic alone. In fact, there are. If this is something that interests you, regardless of whether you're looking to change careers, get a pay rise, quit your job completely, start a business or a side hustle or simply get to know yourself better and discover what fulfils you, there are two books that you absolutely should read: Ashley Stahl's *Your Turn* and John Williams' *Screw Work Break Free* (you can find the links to these books and other recommended resources on my website: www.dominikachoroszko.com/free.)

In my opinion, the two books complement each other really well. The first one goes into detail about discovering who you are and what fulfils you. In contrast, the second one tells you how to get things done more quickly and efficiently whilst showing you some refreshing approaches. Both of them helped me enormously. Therefore, I'll leave this topic to Ashley and John, who will do much better justice than I ever could and get on with the subject I know well: expenses.

Why Bother Tracking Money?

Why bother? Let me answer this question for you:

- You'll be able to excavate some *serious* clutter from your personal finances: overspending, impulse buying and other bad spending habits (*how* much am I spending on coffee?!). It will be there, in black-

and-white, staring you right in the face. Yes, it probably won't be pleasant, but it has to be done if you really want to be in charge of your money.

- You'll know *exactly* where your money is going and have total control over your finances.

- You'll no longer save money 'by accident'. In fact, you'll be able to save up for the things you want intentionally, and you'll know exactly how long it's going to take you.

- You'll be able to tweak things as you go to achieve the outcome you want. If you incur an unexpected expense, you'll be able to 'trim the fat' elsewhere and still hit your savings goal.

- You'll love seeing your debts melt away and your bank account expand consistently. Since I started tracking, I could simply *decide* where I want to channel my money and *do* things like building a solid emergency fund, spending £4k on holiday in the Maldives or sticking £20k into stocks and shares ISA. All planned, no surprises there.

- You'll begin to make your financial decisions from a completely different place – a place of love instead of fear. These decisions will be informed and made out of choice ('I'll wait a month longer and get the thing I really want instead of compromising and getting something mediocre'), and you won't be terrified of running out of money at the end of the month.

Tip

Even if you're already pretty good with your money, there's no harm in trying a new way of doing things. Why? Because you might actually find it easier, more fun and more insightful. There's always something to learn about your spending habits, and there will always be small tweaks you could make, even if you just track for some time.

We talked about the 'why', and I hope you're now pumped up and ready to get your finances organised. Next, let's talk about the 'how'.

How to Track Your Money

You can tame your finances by following the below nine steps.

Step 1: List your spending categories

List all categories you spend money on. Then break each one of them down. It should include anything from your daily expenses like groceries to less frequent ones like your annual car insurance renewal. To get you started, I put together a list of itemised categories that cover most scenarios, but you should remove or add anything that applies to your specific circumstances. One-off or infrequent expenses are marked with an asterisk.

Category	Items	Comments
House & utilities	Rent/mortgage Council tax Electricity & gas Water* Broadband TV licence Paid TV subscription Mobile phone Contents insurance*	Some of these items could be either a monthly expense or be less frequent, so mark it according to your circumstances. For example, water in the UK is billed once every six months, but this could be different if you live elsewhere. Similarly, you might choose to pay your contents insurance as a one-off or monthly payment or choose to pay monthly.
Debt	Repayment 1 Repayment 2	
Groceries	Supermarket 1 Supermarket 2 Supermarket 3 Or Week 1 Week 2 Week 3 Week 4 Or Total groceries	Split your groceries by supermarket. This is my preferred method because you can just stick the whole receipt from each shopping trip under a specific item. Easy. Another option is to split this category by food vs non-food (e.g. toiletries or cleaning products you buy in a supermarket), but I personally find it too faffy to go over each

		receipt and separate it. Nobody has time for that! Unless, of course, you want to figure out precisely how much you spend specifically on food, in which case you can do it for a short period. You could also split your groceries by weeks if you want to stick to a specific weekly target or even just keep adding all of your grocery expenses as one item under 'total' if you're not interested in the details.
Car	Petrol Car wash Car park Car service* Car insurance* MOT* Roadside assistance* Road tax*	
Public transport	Trains Oyster card Taxi	
Cosmetics	Superdrug Boots Item 1 Item 2	I always keep the two major drugstores in my budget because each month, I'll have multiple

		receipts for multiple items from these stores, so it's easy to just add it all up in one place. When you buy items when they run out, such as perfumes, add them as a separate item. At this stage, though, just think of things you buy regularly.
Clothing	Store 1 Store 2 Item 1 Item 2 Item 3 Or Total clothing	Same as cosmetics, this is more of an 'as and when' category, and you can list stores, individual items or even just the total, depending on the purchase. For example, if you placed an online order and bought one jumper, simply add the jumper as your item. If you went to Primark three times in that month and bought loads of little things, there's no point to rewrite your receipt; you'll just add all of your receipts up under 'Primark'.
Hairdresser		
Gifts	Birthday gifts* Christmas gifts*	

Medicine		
Software subscription	Netflix Spotify Anti-virus software* Microsoft package*	
Fitness	Gym Online classes	
Dining out & take away		
Coffee		Yes, I've listed coffee as an entirely separate category because, CHRIST, when left unchecked, those trips to Costa or Starbucks can add up to a small fortune. Speaking from experience here!
Vacation		
Pets	Item 1 Item 2 Item 3	
Other		You should always allocate some 'just in case I need something' money. It could be £20, £50 or even £100 if you can.

Step 2: Create a spreadsheet

Transfer your categories and items onto a spreadsheet. Now, I have tried several budgeting apps but always found some sort of limitations. For example, I wanted my tracking periods to be from payday to payday, as opposed to months, but apps didn't let me customise the labels, which often confused me. Spreadsheets aren't sexy, but you can customise the hell out of them, and that's exactly what you want – something that's easy and quick to use and works for your specific circumstances. The budget template I created already has all categories listed, as well as the formula for all of the calculations you'll need, so if you want to save yourself some setup time, you can download it from www.dominikachoroszko.com/free. Here's an example with just five categories and random numbers to give you an idea of what it should look like:

	Income	Budget	Planned savings	Actual savings
	£2,200	£1,740	£460	£491

	Budget	Spent	Left
	£1,740	£1,709	£31
Housing & utilities	£1,140	£1,140	£0
Rent/ mortgage		£700	
Council tax		£120	
Electricity & gas		£35	
Water		£100	
Broadband		£20	
Mobile phone		£25	
TV licence		£10	
Paid TV subscription		£30	
Contents insurance		£100	
Debt	£100	£100	£0
Loan repayment 1		£70	
Loan repayment 2		£20	
Money borrowed from mum		£10	
Groceries	£350	£305	£45
Tesco		£85	
Waitrose		£120	
Asda		£100	
Car	£50	£35	£15
Petrol		£20	
Car park		£5	
Car wash		£10	
Clothes	£100	£129	-£29
Primark		£54	
M&S jumper		£75	

+ ▦ August ▾

Let's go over the details:

- Each sheet is for one tracking period only: This could be the name of the month, payday date or whatever else works for you. I know some budgets have all twelve months on one sheet. However, this simply shows you the category totals without breaking each one down. An itemised 'per month' layout works best for a few reasons. You will know exactly where your money goes. You won't have to remember what you bought when trying to work out why you spent so much (it will be right in front of you!). And a vertical layout like this is easy to view and edit on a mobile device, meaning you can add expenses on the go.
- Non-recurring expenses: Highlight anything that you won't be paying for regularly. In the above example, I highlighted water and contents insurance as these are paid once or twice a year. Highlighting it makes it easily noticeable, which means you're not going to miss it, and you'll be able to easily budget for it the following year (we'll talk about planning in a bit).
- 'Budget' column: Don't worry about allocating a specific budget for each category in your first month. At this point, you probably don't know how much you're spending, so there's no point pulling a random number just because. For now, leave it at £0. We'll get to it later.
- 'Spent' column: This is where you'll be entering your expenses. Let's say I went to Tesco twice that month and spent £50 on one shopping trip and

£35 on the other. I'll just keep adding all Tesco receipts in that one cell, so the cell would be '=£50+£35'.

- There should be a formula at the top of each category to add up your individual expenses. For example, 'Groceries' came up to £305, and it's the sum of all supermarket expenses.
- 'Left' column: This will be your 'Budget' minus 'Spent', and it will show you whether you have money left or whether you've overspent. However, since we're not defining your budget just yet, ignore this in your first month of tracking.
- 'Income': enter your monthly salary or income in this cell.
- 'Budget' (cell H3): this will be pulling your overall monthly budget from cell B4.
- 'Planned savings': 'Income' minus 'Budget' for the whole month. This is what we've planned will happen.
- 'Actual savings': 'Income' minus 'Spent' (cell G3 – C4). This is what *actually* happened.

Step 3: Make your budget accessible

Upload your spreadsheet to Google Drive or another cloud-based storage solution of choice where you can access your budget from a mobile phone (tip: if you mark it as 'favourite', you'll be able to find it quickly on your Google Drive homepage). You can see how the vertical layout makes it easy to navigate and update your 'Spent' column without having to scroll sideways.

| X | | ↺ ↻ ✥ 🖵 ⋮ | | |

	A	B	C	D	I
2					
3					
4		£1,740	£1,709	£31	
5		Budget	Spent	Left	
6	**Housing & utilities**	£1,140	£1,140	£0	
7	Rent/ mortgage		£700		
8	Council tax		£120		
9	Electricity & gas		£35		
10	Water		£100		
11	Broadband		£20		
12	Mobile phone		£25		
13	TV licence		£10		
14	Paid TV subscription		£30		
15	Contents insurance		£100		
16					
17	**Debt**	£100	£100	£0	
18	Loan repayment 1		£70		
19	Loan repayment 2		£20		
20	Money borrowed from mum		£10		
21					
22	**Groceries**	£350	£305	£45	
23	Tesco		£85		
24	Waitrose		£120		
25	Asda		£100		
26					
27	**Car**	£50	£35	£15	
28	Petrol		£20		
29	Car park		£5		
30	Car wash		£10		
31					

| ≡ | August ▼ | | + |

Step 4: Start collecting your spending data

A few pointers for this step:

- Don't change your spending behaviour at this point. Simply focus on adding everything you spend into your spreadsheet. This is the part where you learn and become aware of your financial clutter.

- In your first month, don't assign any specific targets in your 'Budget' column. Just track what you spend.

- Add your expenses as and when. For example, while waiting for the barista to make your coffee, get your phone out and add it in. You just did your weekly food shopping and loaded everything into the car; add your receipt in before you drive off. You placed an online order for a new kettle; open your spreadsheet and update it. This way, you will never feel like you're managing your money because you're not letting expenses accumulate before you deal with them. You sort it out on the go, and each time, your time investment is approximately ten seconds. Ten seconds plus the 'effort' involved in grabbing your phone is completely worth it if you ask me when the outcome is total control of your money.

- Why not just collect receipts and add it all up at the end of the month? Well, if you've gone over your budget, it's a bit late to fix it, isn't it? Whereas if you track on the go and notice you overspent on one category, you can still get back on track by spending less on another one. Also, this approach does feel like you're managing your money because you'd have to put aside an hour or so every month to enter each receipt, which then becomes a chore.

- I like to add fixed recurring expenses, such as rent or utilities, when creating my budget and before getting billed. You know you have to pay a certain amount each month, so by entering it ahead of time, it's there, accounted for, and you can forget about it.

Step 5: Assign a budget

After the first month, you now know how much you spend and on what. You know what's going on, most likely had a few revelations, and are in a position to plan your annual budget. So for next month, you can start assigning a budget to each category because you'll now know what a realistic target looks like in your case. For example, you've been ordering takeaways a few times a week like it's going out of style, ramping up your 'dining out' spending to £200. You don't have to completely stop ordering takeaways (where's the fun in that!), but you could review that category and decide that ordering food once a week would suffice and lower your target spending to £100. That target seems achievable and has been set based on your spending behaviour. Whereas if you didn't track and had no idea how much you spend on takeaways, you'd likely say, 'Where did all my money go? Okay, from next month, I'm definitely not ordering in anymore.' And you're unlikely to stick with it because the change would be too drastic and for no good reason.

Step 6: Duplicate and amend

Once you assign target spending to each category, duplicate your finished monthly tab and create new tabs for each month till the end of the year.

Step 7: One-off expenses

Remember all the one-off or infrequent expenses you listed in step 1? Go over your annual budget and add them all to the appropriate months. Make adjustments to other categories if needed. Example scenario: Your car insurance and roadside assistance are both due for renewal in October, meaning you're going to have to fork out an additional £600. You still want to save some money, break even or at least minimise the overspend for that month if your income doesn't allow you to stay in the 'green'. You can easily do that by deciding to not spend any money on the following categories (or at least reduce the target budget): dining out, coffee, clothing, cosmetics, hairdresser and 'other'.

If you're still convinced that tracking expenses is boring, focus on all the energy you'll be freeing up by not worrying about how much money you have left over. Think of the freedom and empowerment you'll gain from it.

Step 8: Savings

Create a thirteenth tab and add up 'Planned savings' from all tabs (cells I3). Doing this will tell you how much you'll save this year if you stick to your budget! Then do the same for 'Actual savings' (cells J3). You'll be able to check this number at the end of the year to see how much you saved.

Step 9: Forecast

After a year of tracking, you'll have twelve months of your *actual* spending and saving data! How cool is that! So now, at the end of the year, make a copy of the whole document and prepare a forecast for next year. Update your income if it changes, remove your spending numbers and adjust the target budget if needed. This will only take you an hour or so, and you'll have a plan for the whole of next year!

Why the Method Works

Tracking your money on the go using this simple format works because it takes almost no time, so it doesn't feel like a chore. Yes, nine steps seem like a lot, but you only need one or two hours for the initial one-off setup, then ten seconds here and there throughout the year and then another hour or so to create a budget for the following year. That's it. And each year after that, it gets even better because you won't have the one-off setup anymore. And that quick, easy and simple method gives you more benefits than you could ask for.

Your bad spending habits are decluttered, your money is organised and basically on autopilot. You have full awareness and total control over what's going on in your personal finances.

And you know what the best thing is? Once your money begins doing what you want it to do, you will start feeling excited and want to push it even further. You might start thinking: *Can I save even more? Can I make it work harder for me? Can I invest it somehow?'* It becomes a fun and intentional way of living, not just a New Year's resolution which dies after one month of collecting receipts.

Saving Tips

I am absolutely and utterly against extreme frugality unless your current (and temporary!) situation means you have to, and as you know, I've been there. I don't endorse an extremely restrictive lifestyle, couponing or watching every single penny because life is simply too short for that. (When I say couponing, I don't mean using an occasional 30 per cent off discount code on an Uber. I'm referring to those guys who dedicate their whole days to combing through store magazines and then spending £1000 worth of coupons on excessive amounts of crap that (a) clutters their pantries, (b) they don't even like. Grinds my gears. But there are ways you could save which don't require much effort and money going out of your bank account that simply doesn't have to. The good thing is one phone call or webchat could easily fix it. Here are tricks I personally use or have used to keep my expenses down:

Before buying stuff, think of clutter

Ask yourself: Do I value this item more than the space in my home? Do I need it? How badly do I want it? Personally, I stopped buying things I wasn't 100 per cent sure I wanted. If I like something, but it doesn't take my breath away, I don't buy it. If I'm about 80 per cent convinced I want it, I wait a day or two, and in the vast majority of cases, I no longer want it. But if I still do, then I buy it.

Shop around

Check out the best deals for TV, broadband, mobile phones and utilities when your contract is due to end. New customers always tend to get better deals, so in this case, it doesn't pay off to be loyal. You can save yourself hundreds of pounds just by clicking a few buttons or going on a live chat (introverts' favourite). You'll either get a better deal from your existing company to stop you from leaving, or you can switch and get a cheaper deal with another provider.

Avoid finance

I never ever bought a car on finance because I hate the idea of lingering repayments and paying interest – yuk! And if you do a bit of research, you can find some amazing deals out there. For example, I bought a used five-year-old Mercedes A-Class with only 35,000 miles on it for £4,500. It seemed like a great car and had been well cared for. Still, hey, you can never be 100 per cent certain, so I also brought a mechanic with me to properly check the car. (If you don't know a mechanic, you can pay for a vehicle inspection service offered by most motoring organisations.) I followed the same process with my next car, and both of them served me well for many, many years. So my advice is to save up and buy a car in cash. It will save you a ton of money.

Tip

Speaking of cars, always negotiate your roadside assistance (I've never paid a full price) and car insurance. All it takes is a phone call, asking if they have any available discounts. If not – shop around, and I promise you'll find better deals.

Review auto-renew subscriptions

To give you an example, I purchased an anti-virus software for £12 for the whole year. Eleven months later, I got an email informing me the auto-renewal price was £85. My first thought was: *You've got to be kidding me.* My second thought: *Screw you.* I immediately disabled the auto-renew (which in a blink of an eye prompted them to throw discounts at me) and found the exact same software online for a fraction of the price (a legit retailer, not a dodgy site). *Ka-ching!*

Speaking of subscriptions, do you use all of them regularly? Most of us have Netflix, but how often do we actually watch it? Their pricing is low enough for it to go under the radar (£5.99 for the cheapest plan at writing), and most people can't be bothered to cancel it, even when they aren't watching it. But that's £71.88 over the year that just goes down the drain. Their cancellation process is quick, and it's also easy to restart your membership, so my advice is to pay only for the months when there's something you genuinely want to watch.

Home improvements on your rental

If you're a renter, offer to carry out small home improvements in return for lowering your rent. Whether you're moving into a new rental property or planning to stay in the current one, chances are, most properties could do with a lick of paint. To get a professional to do the painting could cost thousands of pounds, so it could be a win-win for you and the landlord if you offer to do it yourself. Bear in mind they will likely add a clause in your contract specifying the allowed colour palette (probably 'neutral') and saying that they will charge you if you do a terrible job and utterly mess up the property, which is fair enough. Painting is just one example, and there will be other small DIY tasks you could do in your rented home.

Watch out for rent increases

To give you an example, my ex-boyfriend and I rented this beautiful, modern new-built apartment. However, shortly after we moved in, things started to happen . . . The toilet was stealthily leaking, causing mould, and there was a 'yummy' yellow stain in the bedroom. The oven almost fell out on my feet the first time I used it because, as it turned out, it wasn't even attached. A bedroom window was installed upside down, and one of the corners wasn't attached at all, meaning we could never actually open it for fear that it would fall out eventually.

After a year, we received the contract renewal, notifying us about a rent increase. I laughed and wrote a long email, politely explaining why I thought a rent increase couldn't be justified, listing all the problems we had dealt with. To my surprise, they responded favourably and never actually increased the rent - not only just in that one year! So the lesson is: don't be afraid to question things. The outcome might surprise you.

Prioritise

Figure out what's important to you and offset it somewhere else. I keep seeing articles, usually in newspapers or magazines, with headlines such as 'An unemployed single mum of 10 feeds the whole family for £10 a week'. I'm obviously exaggerating, but you know the type of articles I'm referring to. But as someone who spends a lot of money in supermarkets, it made me wonder whether I could reduce this somehow. That's when I did a thorough audit and split my 'supermarket' budget category into weeks and also food versus non-food to really understand where my money was going. Turns out I could downgrade some of my household products (toilet roll, chemicals, etc.), but not food, as I wasn't willing to compromise on quality. However, I offset this in another category - 'dining out', mainly takeaways. Since I really enjoy homemade food, I rarely order takeaways, which actually saves me a lot of money. Despite spending so much in supermarkets,

I'm still saving, so I'm cool with that. So work out what's important to you and prioritise it in your budget. As Joe Biden said:

'Don't tell me what you value, show me your budget, and I'll tell you what you value.'

Sign up for the Money Saving Expert newsletter

There is a lot of information there, and most of it won't be relevant, but when I get one of those, I just scan the headlines to see if anything there interests me. And every now and then, there will be a golden nugget. For example, I learned about the 'working from home tax relief' from the MSE newsletter. If you haven't heard of it, it basically allows you to pay less tax if you had to work from home due to Covid. And the good thing is, the tax relief is valid for a whole year, even if you only worked from home for one day! It wasn't much – approximately £10 a month – but that was roughly the amount my utility bills increased since I started working from home, so this was perfect! The newsletter also has a lot of useful updates and deals for utility providers, so it's definitely worth signing up.

Memberships

Do you really need a gym membership? Now, I do love a heavy-ass barbell, but during the lockdown, I was forced to find other ways. There are, in fact, so many amazing free resources online (I've included them all in your free download) that I don't think I'll ever fully go back to the gym. For some of them, you might need a pull-up bar or a couple of sets of dumbbells, which is a one-off cost that will save you money in the long run. For others, you only need your own body weight, and these exercises actually tend to be the hardest! And whilst training at home for over a year and a half now, I have not lost muscle mass or put on extra body fat, so it's definitely working! If you love the gym atmosphere, you could combine home workouts with one or two sessions in a pay-as-you-go gym. Some single-entry passes can cost as little as £5.

Alternatively, if you truly love the gym, use it multiple times a week, and don't want to give it up, see if you could downgrade it. Swap David Lloyd for The Gym and save yourself a ton of cash.

Look for discounts

Check if your workplace offers discounts. Many companies provide various benefits, cashback or discounts for many retailers, but most people tend to forget about it! As much as I can't be bothered to look for Wilko vouchers when I'm only going to get £10 worth of household products, it's worth looking into when you're planning a bigger purchase. For example, I found an IKEA discount that saved me about £250. Other categories worth looking into are car insurance, roadside assistance and electronics, which came in handy when I bought a new TV and a laptop.

I hope the above saving tips help you to easily reduce unnecessary expenses rather than feel overly restrictive! The bottom line is:

As long as you're still saving the amount of money you want, it's okay to enjoy life – that's ultimately what money is for!

And when you have a budget, it's very easy to see whether you can afford to do that or not. If you can't, then you might have to tighten your belt for a while as you're working on improving your financial situation. It's all about evaluating your current circumstances.

Enjoying Your Newfound Wealth

I have no doubt that once you start tracking your expenses and tweaking your budget to stay on track, you'll find extra money which would have previously just vanished from your account. So what should you do with it? If you have relatively small debt, I recommend prioritising paying that off. After that, I'd start saving up for an emergency fund. This should ideally be at least three to six months' worth of your expenses and stashed away somewhere you can access it easily if you need to. The emergency fund should only ever be used for emergencies. Things like your car broke down, you need to replace a washing machine, or you lost your job and need to stay afloat until you find a new one. A holiday or a new handbag is, sadly, not an emergency.

If you have a lot of debt that will take a long time to pay off, I'd recommend combining paying it off and saving up for an emergency fund (whilst simultaneously increasing your income). Why? Because the longer you wait to put money aside, the higher the chances that something eventually will go wrong; you can't just assume that you'll never have any emergencies for, say, five years! And if something does go wrong, the last thing you want is to be forced to take on even more debt to cover that.

Once you've paid off your debt and built an emergency fund, it's a good time to consider investing. Why? Because the only thing your money will do when stashed in a sock/savings account (the same thing these days) is get eroded by inflation. Whereas money invested in shares has the potential to grow.

Now, many women have this perception that it's a 'boy thing' or that investing is difficult, and in the beginning, I also felt intimidated by the whole thing. But by now, you should know how to tackle all of the big, scary and overwhelming things - one tiny step at a time (*Iron Man!*). And the first action I took was to Google 'how to invest'. As I read more and more articles, I'd have more questions and search for more answers. I looked for articles written in plain and simple language to make the learning process easier and more enjoyable.

I'm not a financial advisor, so I won't tell you what to do, but I encourage you to simply do a bit of research to see whether investing could potentially be suitable for you. A few good starting points to search for include:

- Stocks & Shares ISA (an account where each year in the UK, you're allowed to put up to £20k in, and you don't pay taxes on any gains you make from your investments)

- Diversification (spreading your money across several different stocks in various industries, geographical locations or other categories to minimise the risk)

- Trading platforms (you need to actually buy your shares somewhere, and trading platforms, such as Interactive Investor or Hargreaves Lansdown, are the equivalent of stock 'supermarkets' – you can open several accounts with them, including Stocks & Shares ISA).

On top of learning about investments, different companies and their financials, I also signed up for a paid share recommendations newsletter. I figured that it's worth paying around £150 a year for regular recommendations from professional analysts. They really detail why they believe a company is worth investing in and cover business, financials, valuation, management, potential risks, etc. Of course, it's impossible to invest in all of these recommendations, so I'd normally read each analysis and then invest in stocks that resonated with me the most.

Now, I'm certainly no Warren Buffett. Still, I went from knowing absolutely nothing about investing to owning a solid portfolio of about thirty stocks which increased its value by 50 per cent in a year. I believe that you can do it, too, if you commit to educating yourself little by little.

Credit Card or Not?

I got a credit card when I was at university, but it took me a long time to make that decision because I was terrified of debt. However, my bank manager eventually convinced me to get it, and I'm glad she did. She explained that as long as I paid everything off at the end of the month, I wouldn't incur any charges, but it would benefit me in terms of protection when shopping online and help with building a credit score. And I did, in fact, benefit from both.

One factor that affects your credit score, aka your 'financial health,' is how reliable you are when paying off debt. Your credit score matters because it helps you get approved for things like a mortgage, renting a property, getting a mobile phone contract and much more. And according to Experian,[15] some of the best ways to increase your credit score include monitoring the amounts owed (the lower, the better), building a good payment history (not missing payments) and having a long credit history (the longer, the better). With that in mind, I started putting all of my online purchases on my credit card instead of paying from my current account and making regular repayments throughout the month. I never bought anything that I didn't have the money for in my current account, meaning that I never actually used my credit card for debt. Just with that one credit card, I got to the highest possible credit score of 999.

The importance of that one credit card became even more apparent when I was moving homes. Due to a system delay in updating the new address information, the credit card disappeared from my Experian account. The result? My credit score plummeted from 999, in the 'Excellent' range, to around 780, in the 'Fair' range. That's two levels lower! I don't know whether there were other factors, but the only difference I could see was that one credit card didn't get picked up, meaning Experian thought I didn't have any credit history. As soon as the issue was fixed and my credit card became visible again, my credit score returned to a glowing 999.

I also mentioned payment protection when shopping online. At the time of writing, when you use your credit card and spend over £100, your credit card company becomes jointly liable if something goes wrong with your purchase; read up on Section 75 of the Consumer Credit Act for more information. This comes in really handy if you have a problem with a retailer. A while ago, I purchased an office desk online and paid for express delivery because I needed it quite urgently. A couple of days after I placed the order, I received a generic email from them telling me that they had stock issues and the desk would be delivered . . . in *four months*. Convinced that it was a typo, I messaged them and tried to call, but no luck. Shortly after that, I received another impersonal auto-email with a new delivery date – this time, in six months. I was done dealing with this company and asked for a refund. Of course, no response (rude). It was then that I decided to take that Section 75 for a spin and see what could be done. All I had to do was go on my bank's website, fill in a short form and receive a refund within a couple of days.

So, in my opinion, yes, a credit card can be a great tool for building your financial health and for adding extra protection, providing you don't use it for buying shit you can't afford.

You should see by now that the same decluttering and organisation formula works for any given area, including finances. It doesn't have to be unnecessarily complicated. Simply:

Bring awareness to the present situation, weed out what's not working and create a new structure that supports your desire - and you'll be on your way to achieving your goal.

Chapter 14

Bringing It All Together: Space, Mind and Finances

This is where it gets really interesting, and your money, mindset and space organisation habits become intertwined. Examining these three areas without judgement can be a source of incredibly valuable insight into yourself.

Your mindset can drive you or prevent you from doing things, and it's no different with money. Until you tackle what's in your head, it will be difficult to make lasting changes.

I want you to really think about those habits and beliefs that relate to money somehow and don't make you feel good. Let's take hoarding as an example. Keeping clutter might seem irrelevant, but in many cases, it highlights a scarcity mindset; we talked about decluttering being perceived by some as a 'waste of money' in Chapter 2 (*see* Letting Go of Your Emotional Attachment to Stuff). If you fall into this category, I encourage you to grab a journal or your laptop and free-write on the topic of keeping clutter in the context of money because writing tends to unlock some juicy insights. Write down anything that comes to mind that will help you get to the root cause of your problem.

- Are you keeping stuff because you're worried that you won't have enough and will have to spend money to replace the items you discarded?

- Has something happened in your childhood to make you feel that way?

- Are you worried that you'd look 'poor' if you had fewer belongings?

- Why are you still holding on to that jar of Cajun seasoning, which expired eight years ago and could be replaced for £1.25 (or not replaced at all, since you haven't used it for almost a decade)?

It might take a few goes to get the insights you're after, but once you have your 'aha!' moment, use the techniques from Chapter 9, Taking Action on Your Mental Clutter, to tackle it. In this scenario, you could reframe your thoughts about holding on to clutter, examine what the loving decision should look like instead of being driven by the fear of not having enough, and visualise yourself living in a beautiful, uncluttered home and feeling extra abundant.

Now, examine your spending habits and pinpoint the ones that deep down don't make you feel good. Do you ever buy yourself expensive treats? The activity itself is neither good nor bad. It's what drives you that makes a difference. Have you got your emergency fund sorted and enough buffer in your savings that getting that pair of shoes won't get you into trouble (abundant spending, filled with joy and excitement)? Or are you broke and put the shoes on your credit card (wasteful spending, driven by ego to *look* abundant, filled with fear and guilt)? If it was the latter:

- Why did you do that, knowing well that spending this money would put you in an even worse financial position?

- Do you feel so overwhelmed with the current situation that you've given up on trying to fix it?

- Were your parents always in debt, and you grew up thinking that 'this is just what happens'?

On the other end of the spectrum, we've got penny-pinching. Would you rather wait two weeks to get your parcel delivered instead of paying an extra £2 for express delivery?

- Does the thought of spending money 'unnecessarily' make you feel sick? Why do you think that is?

- Do you believe that you have to hoard every penny because you'll never earn enough to justify that?

Since we're on the topic of income, are you currently stuck at some imaginary maximum setpoint and don't believe that you could ever earn more? You could be cutting out flat whites from your budget until the cows come home. Still, until you start believing in your earning abilities, there'll only be so much you can save, so it's incredibly important to tackle the parts of your money mindset that are holding you back.

Let me give you a few examples of common misconceptions that relate to money in some way and how you could reframe them:

Old thought	New thought
I hate my job, and I can't think of anything worse than climbing up the corporate ladder. So I'm stuck at my current income level forever.	I can get more money, but not in my current field. If I want to work in a job that really interests me, I can change careers if I take small daily steps to get there. It's never too late to create change. Plus, I'd rather give it a go because good things might just happen rather than be stuck in a job I hate forever. (I personally know someone who went from training engineers on how to install satellite dishes and comply with health and safety regulations to working in technology. Before he got that job, he knew *nothing* about the industry and had no work experience. But because this was what he wanted, he made it a priority to learn, network and study for relevant qualifications for almost two years, which resulted in him landing the dream job. Oh, and have I mentioned the substantial salary increase that came with it?! So yes, it's possible.)

Throwing stuff away is a waste of money.	Well, that's BS because I currently have four boxes of lightbulbs just because I couldn't find any in all that mess. I must have spent a fortune 'replacing' things that are, in fact, hiding in my home somewhere! (Fun fact: Disorganisation results in 23 per cent of adults paying their bills late and incurring late payment fees, according to Harris Interactive study.[16] So think about that next time you catch yourself making excuses for keeping that pair of old socks which has been sewn up a few times already!)
I'm in too much debt. What's the point of even trying to get out of it? It will never happen.	I will get out of it, but it will take time, so I need to be patient. Meanwhile, I will stop adding more debt, I will take control of my expenses by consistently tracking them, and I will explore different ways to earn more money. The possibilities are endless, and I already feel energised to get started!
If I want more money, I'll need to work harder and do more hours, and I can't be arsed.	If that was the case, cleaners and retail workers would be the richest people in the world. Getting a promotion doesn't necessarily mean working longer hours or harder; I will have *different* responsibilities. I also have enough experience now to work *smarter*. I know when to question things and refuse to take on a new project.

Your current money situation, whether it's good or bad, is a result of your past beliefs about income and expenses. That's why reviewing and decluttering your money mindset is important if you wish to make changes in this area.

Fortunately, mindset isn't a fixed thing that you're just stuck with for life. In fact, in her research, Carol Dweck found higher levels of achievement are linked to a growth mindset (believing that success is based on hard work and learning) as opposed to a fixed mindset (believing that success is based on innate abilities and talent).[17] If you dedicate time and put work in, you'll get the results. Refer to Chapter 7, Becoming Aware of Mental Clutter, and, if you haven't already, focus on becoming aware of any messy money issues. After that, choose techniques I shared in Chapter 9, Taking Action on Your Mental Clutter and Chapter 10, Dreaming Up Success, to address them.

Once you understand what's really holding you back and start taking tiny consistent steps toward changing your money mindset, your financial situation will improve with time.

Gratitude for Bills

There was a time when every time I saw a bank notification pop up on my phone, reminding me that direct debit for a bill of some sort was due, I used to roll my eyes, which was more often than not accompanied by a loud 'Oh for

FUCK's sake!' And you know what that did? Other than making me feel annoyed, not much. Bills tend to have a bad reputation, and most people complain about them. The thing is – you *have to* pay them. So by moaning about something that you know for a fact is not going to go away, the only person that suffers is *you*. Yes, you should always shop around and get the best deals you possibly can, but once that's done, just accept that if you want to enjoy the benefits of electricity, you're going to have to pay for it.

We tend to see utility bills are something 'not fun'. But don't you have fun watching TV? Or taking long hot baths? Or having Zoom calls with your friends? None of these things would be possible if it wasn't for the 'boring' services you pay for.

Remember the gratitude exercise from Chapter 9 (*see* Gratitude and Appreciation)? I want you to do something similar, but specifically in the context of bills. Think of all the bills you're currently paying and reasons why you're grateful for it. Feel free to write it down in your journal or just reflect on it. Here are some of my examples to get you started:

- Rent/mortgage – I'm so grateful for such a beautiful apartment for a very reasonable price. I definitely lucked out here!

- Broadband – I'm so grateful for it because it allows me to access the internet, take online courses and learn from the comfort of my home, watch YouTube videos on my TV, access social media on my phone, and so much more!

- Mobile phone – I'm grateful for it because I can keep in touch with my loved ones, take beautiful pictures and browse on the go, wherever I am.

- Investing platform fee – thanks to this platform, my money gets to grow so much for a tiny monthly fee!

- Spotify – it gives me access to all the wonderful podcasts which consistently provide support on my personal development journey.

- Gas, electricity and water bills – without paying for these things, virtually *nothing* in my home would function, so I'm very grateful for it!

Each time you complain about paying for something, ask yourself why. Is this something that you can really do without? If so, cancel it. But if it is, in fact, benefiting you in many ways, be grateful for it.

Final Words

When you eliminate or even reduce the feelings associated with clutter, such as anxiety, helplessness, lack of energy, 'stuckness' or overwhelm, there's a whole new world of possibilities that will open in front of you. Why? Because when you tackle all the different types of clutter, you'll gain more *physical space, time, money and mental clarity*. And these four things can be life-changing. So let's just think for a minute about all the new and exciting things you will be able to replace clutter with.

Invite People Over

It's not uncommon for clutter to make us feel embarrassed and reluctant to have guests over. In the past, you may have also experienced the sheer terror of a family member announcing their imminent arrival, and all you could do was panic because you needed to magically get the house into a reasonable state. When you don't have clutter, though, things become easy. You could spontaneously invite a friend over or plan a 'girls' night in'. Unexpected family visits also won't be stressful anymore (at least from the home perspective) as all you'll need to do is a quick 'maintenance' tidy-up.

Focus on Your Exercise, Diet and Wellbeing

Healthy eating and exercise might not be at the forefront of your mind when your home is filled with clutter, particularly the kitchen. But once you have the physical space, more time and more money, you can actually take some 'me time' and prioritise your wellbeing.

There are so many activities you could actually do at home when you have space! The options include weightlifting, yoga, Pilates, aerobics, callisthenics, flexibility training and much more. In most cases, you won't even need much equipment – just space! You might want to get a couple of dumbbells and maybe a pull-up bar, which is a versatile tool for training the upper body and abs. These days you can get pull-up bars that can be folded flat and hung in your wardrobe or stored behind the door, so you don't end up with an awkward piece of equipment when you're not using it! Plus, there are some really amazing follow-along training videos online, which I've included on www.dominikachoroszko.com/free, together with handy equipment that won't clutter your space.

Create a Productive Office Space

Clutter is known to cause distraction and reduce productivity. This sucks, particularly in your office area, which should inspire productivity and creativity instead of killing it! A tidy office space might be just what you need to start reading more, do online courses on the subject that interests you or even start a side hustle.

Upgrade Your Career/Find Your True Passion

Most of us are held back by some beliefs that we picked up along the way from other people or society. Our careers and financial wellbeing are often heavily affected. But the work we did clearing all the mindset clutter is meant to help you move past it. Imagine the possibilities that lie ahead when you start believing in yourself and pursuing your dreams. This could mean you finally apply for that job you didn't believe you deserved, change careers or completely ditch working for someone else and start your own business. It's all possible, and it all begins with your mindset.

Treat Yourself

It's natural for many of us to spend money on everything and everybody other than ourselves. Having some extra cash (no physical clutter + better money management = not buying duplicates, less laundry, lower bills, better spending habits) combined with a more positive mindset means that you will be able to finally prioritise yourself. You deserve it! So what is that thing you've been dreaming of? What have you wanted to buy for yourself but never did because it was 'too expensive', 'a waste of money' or made you feel guilty for even wanting it?

Add Character to Your Place

Wouldn't it be amazing to transform your home from simply functional to something truly 'you'? With clutter filling your home to the brim, decorating was probably the last thing on your mind. But with all that clutter gone, you can finally be creative and put a stamp on your place. These little details, splashes of colour, clean walls and bits of décor that bring a smile to your face is what transforms your four walls into that oasis of calm you've always wanted.

Start Dating

The benefits of living clutter-free are truly compound. This is why I believe it's a holistic philosophy rather than an isolated act of purging only physical stuff. Clearing each area of your life matters, and improvements in one stimulate further improvements in another.

Maybe you've been shying away from dating because you had too much on your plate, felt embarrassed about the state of your house or just felt too overwhelmed to even think about it. But imagine the new you: prioritising yourself, taking time to exercise and improve your nutrition, living in an enviable home full of space and filled with light, someone who's energised, more confident, empowered and has boundaries. Someone who just oozes that energy that magnetises people around you. I think it's safe to say that it's a far better place to explore dating if that's what you choose to do.

Spend Quality Time with Your Family

I've seen places where families cannot eat together or play with the kids because their homes are too cluttered to accommodate these simple activities. A clear and clutter-free space solves these problems. Physical things are just stuff. It means very little without the people you love. Getting rid of your excess possessions will enrich your life by allowing you to spend quality time with your loved ones, resulting in a more fulfilled, happier life.

Do More Things That Are Good for Your Soul

It's important to include playtime in our lives. If we make it all about work and chores, where's the fun in that? A clutter-free place combined with extra money allows you to pursue hobbies and implement self-care routines you may have previously dismissed due to the lack of space. Did you dream about learning an instrument? Writing a book? Setting up a beauty and nail station? Getting a pet? Or perhaps learning to bake fancy cakes? A clutter-free environment enables you to easily sprinkle some of that joy into your life.

To end, I want to leave you with a cheat sheet of the process over the page, which you can quickly refer to. Remember that this can be applied to any other area, not just the three below. I sincerely hope you found the advice in this book helpful and wish you a happier, calmer and more relaxed life. And if you enjoyed this book, please leave me a review on Amazon and come find me on social media.

Dominika
www.dominikachoroszko.com
www.instagram.com/theorganisedintrovert

Declutter Space, Mind and Finances Cheat Sheet

	Audit of the present situation (identify clutter)	Get rid of what's not needed (purge clutter)	Create a structure for what you've kept (organise)
Physical space	Become aware of *why* you're holding on to so much stuff. Find out exactly what you have. Ensure that there isn't anything hidden in your drawers that you're not aware of.	Throw away, give away, donate or sell belongings that you no longer need or love.	Organise your belongings in a way that keeps them tidy. Every item has its designated place, it's easily accessible, and you know where it is.

Mindset	Become aware of thoughts that don't feel good and aren't working in your favour.	Get rid of limiting beliefs, thoughts and habits that make you feel bad by, for example, reframing negative thoughts or conducting a negativity detox.	Implement a routine that keeps you on track, such as regular affirmations, meditation or allowing time for gratitude.
Personal finances	Become aware of your current money habits by tracking your spending and income to have actual data showing your current situation.	Eliminate unnecessary expenses and spending habits. Get rid of any false beliefs about money, such as your perceived inability to earn more.	Implement a budget that keeps you on track. Plan your monthly and annual savings and assign a set amount of money to each category in your budget.

About the Author

Dominika is a decluttering and organisation expert, a life coach and a former world-class ballroom dancer with a keen aesthetic eye. After almost two decades of decluttering, organising, finessing her methods and applying them to different areas of life, she now helps her clients create more space – both on the inside and outside.

Notes

[1] Bourg Carter, S. (14 March 2012). 'Why Mess Causes Stress: 8 Reasons, 8 Remedies'. Psychology Today. Retrieved 13 December 2021: https://www.psychologytoday.com/gb/blog/high-octane-women/201203/why-mess-causes-stress-8-reasons-8-remedies

[2] Organized Interiors. '35 Surprising Home Organization Statistics That'll Inspire You to Tidy Up'. Organized Interiors. Retrieved 13 December 2021: https://www.organizedinteriors.com/blog/home-organization-statistics/

[3] Daily Mail Reporter. (21 March 2012). 'Lost Something Already Today? Misplaced items cost us ten minutes a day'. Daily Mail Online. Retrieved 13 December 2021: https://www.dailymail.co.uk/news/article-2117987/Lost-today-Misplaced-items-cost-minutes-day.html

[4] Wade P.J. (13 March 2000). 'Not tonight Dear, I'm Cleaning the Closet'. *Realty Times*. Retrieved 13 December 2021: https://realtytimes.com/archives/item/20629-20000314_closet

[5] Organized Interiors. '35 Surprising Home Organization Statistics That'll Inspire You to Tidy Up'. Organized Interiors. Retrieved 20 December 2021: https://www.organizedinteriors.com/blog/home-organization-statistics/

[6] Proctor, B. (2019). *12 Power Principles for Success*. G&D Media.

[7] Proctor, B. (2019). *12 Power Principles for Success*. G&D Media.

[8] Pira, A. (2019). *Homeless to Billionaire: The 18 Principles of Wealth Attraction and Creating Unlimited Opportunity*. Forbes Books

[9] Sarno, J.E. (2018). *Healing Back Pain (Reissue Edition): The Mind-Body Connection*. Grand Central Publishing.

[10] Gordon, A. (20 July 2017). 'Somatic Tracking'. The Mindbody Syndrome (TMS) Discussion Forum. Retrieved 13 December 2021: https://www.tmswiki.org/forum/threads/day-9-somatic-tracking.16532/

[11] Pira, A. (2019). *Homeless to Billionaire: The 18 Principles of Wealth Attraction and Creating Unlimited Opportunity*. Forbes Books.

[12] Hurst, K. 'Celebrities and the Law of Attraction'. TheLawofAttraction.com. Retrieved 13 December 2021: https://www.thelawofattraction.com/celebrities-law-attraction/

[13] The Joe Rogan Experience MMA Show. (9 February 2021). 'JRE MMA Show #99 with Francis Ngannou'. Spotify. Retrieved 13 December 2021: https://open.spotify.com/episode/6h2N6q4gUZ32z1IsvyXFKh

[14] Stahl, A. (2021). *You Turn: Get Unstuck, Discover Your Direction, and Design Your Dream Career*. Benbella Books.

[15] Experian. 'What Affects Your Credit Score'. Retrieved 13 December 2021: https://www.experian.com/blogs/ask-experian/credit-education/score-basics/what-affects-your-credit-scores/

[16] Organized Interiors. '35 Surprising Home Organization Statistics That'll Inspire You to Tidy Up'. Retrieved 13 December 2021: https://www.organizedinteriors.com/blog/home-organization-statistics/

[17] Dweck, C. (2007). *Mindset: The New Psychology of Success*. Ballantine Books.

Made in the USA
Las Vegas, NV
03 May 2023

71455383R00125